# RESCU

# RESCUED BY LOVE

Jenny Davis

**HODDER & STOUGHTON**
LONDON SYDNEY AUCKLAND TORONTO

Prayers on page 113 are reproduced from *The Alternative Service Book 1980* by permission of the Central Board of Finance of the Church of England.

**British Library Cataloguing in Publication Data**
Davis, Jenny
  Rescued by love.
  1. Christian life – Biographies
  I. Title
  248.4092

ISBN 0–340–54058–3

*Published by Hodder and Stoughton, a division of Hodder and Stoughton Ltd, Mill Road, Dunton Green, Sevenoaks, Kent TN13 2YA. Editorial Office: 47 Bedford Square, London WC1B 3DP.*

*Photoset by Chippendale Type Ltd., Otley, West Yorkshire.*

*Printed in Great Britain by Cox & Wyman Ltd., Reading.*

## Love

Love bade me welcome; yet my soul drew back,
    Guilty of dust and sin.
But quick-ey'd Love, observing me grow slack
    From my first entrance in,
Drew nearer to me, sweetly questioning
    If I lack'd anything.

'A guest,' I answer'd, 'worthy to be here';
    Love said, 'You shall be he.'
'I, the unkind, ungrateful? Ah, my dear,
    I cannot look on Thee.'
Love took my hand, and smiling did reply,
    'Who made the eyes but I?'

'Truth, Lord; but I have marr'd them; let my shame
    Go where it doth deserve.'
'And know you not,' says Love, 'who bore the
    blame?'
    'My dear, then I will serve.'
'You must sit down,' says Love, 'and taste My meat.'
    So I did sit and eat.

*George Herbert 1593–1633*

# CONTENTS

# INTRODUCTION

When I came out of prison, many people, including my own children, asked me to write about my experiences, my feelings and reactions – not for sensational reasons, but so that others going through something similar or any form of suffering might take heart and be encouraged not to lose hope. At that time, I think I was too close to the situation and too emotionally involved to write with a clear and level head. Since then, seven years have passed, giving me enough space, I think, to develop sufficient objectivity about events. Had I written sooner, I might have focused too much on crusading for those caught up in our penal system.

As it is, I have had a wider brief in mind: to try to show those caught up in the ugliness of life, the confused, the despairing, and those whose lives are full of pain and bitterness, that through Jesus Christ there is beauty and light, hope and healing for them.

In selecting what to share in this book, my main concern has been to focus on my struggle through the darkness and into the light of God's love. The other guideline has been to cause those I love as little pain as possible. This accounts for some of the areas that I omit or say very little about. However, I have, with the loving help of family, friends and my spiritual counsellor, looked at these matters and they have been dealt with, healed and put behind me. For if God offers us forgiveness, we must learn to forgive ourselves, and lay down that particular burden of guilt for ever. It is not possible to experience the freedom of love that God offers if we continue to drag guilt around with us like unwanted luggage.

I acknowledge my indebtedness to Margaret Magdalen for her book *Transformed by Love*, which has been a great inspiration to me, and confirmed my own thinking on the joy of forgiveness. I would also like to thank her for the support of her written encouragement.

I offer this book in gratitude to all with whom I lived in prison, for their love, support, encouragement and acceptance. They showed me the face of Christ. I cannot name them, but there was a light in each one, and I love them all.

I also dedicate this book to those who support me now – my family and friends. Thank you to all who have encouraged me in the writing of it. A special thank you to Jean Watson who patiently helped, guided and advised me throughout; no easy task with an autobiography of this nature.

If through reading what I have written just one person were to recognise his or her need and be similarly rescued by love, I should be happy.

# FOREWORD

Without forgiveness there is no love.
Without love there is no growth.
Without growth there is no continuing life.

*Esther de Waal*

When I married Christopher, I was deeply in love with him. The thought of spending the rest of my life with him at my side gave me a sense of happiness and security that seemed to make everything complete. If anyone had told me then that one day I would take his life, I should have looked at them with utter disbelief. Yet this is what happened.

What went wrong with a relationship to such an extent that I was able to turn round and shoot the person I loved the most? Grief, born out of a desperation to put things right, became the trigger. How can love destroy love? I can only use my own experience to answer that question, by saying love can be misplaced, distorted and misused.

I am not alone in having such pent-up emotions. Many of us who live quietly, trying to hide our hurts and emotions behind stiff upper lips, are the ones most likely to break. We can break in many ways; at the extreme end, we may turn to alcohol, drugs, suicide, murder or manslaughter. Whatever society believes about these reactions, we are often left with a sense of guilt or remorse for the rest of our lives or, even worse, totally destroyed by our experiences.

This would have happened to me if I had not been rescued by love. Margaret Magdalen CSMV in her book *Transformed by Love (DLT,* 1989) says much of sin is the misuse of good. Love is good but, distorted, it can turn in on itself and become destructive and evil. However, since God's love and mercy are beyond human understanding, whatever we do or think in our lives, whatever wrongs we commit until the day we die, if we turn to God and ask with complete sincerity for forgiveness, we are forgiven, healed and set free. This is Christ's promise which, through his grace, I have found to be true in my own life.

True love enfolds all other emotions. It gives a freedom of expression which, being grounded in reality, takes into account our frailty and vulnerability, acknowledging that we are not, nor ever can be, perfect.

Because true love is a total commitment, it understands that anger, resentment, hurt and suffering are part of being human. It is kind and gentle, accepting and rejoicing in joy and peace, but also ready to defuse and live through violence and hurt with forgiveness. The truest love is found within God's love which encompasses all things.

# 1

# Childhood

I, a stranger and afraid
In a world I never made.
                              *A.E. Housman*


People make all kinds of assumptions about the effects of childhood. It is often taken for granted, for example, that if a child comes from a broken home or experiences some other tragedy, he or she will have a poor outlook on life. But this is not necessarily so: difficulties can be a means of strengthening people.

I was born in a nursing home in Ascot, Berkshire on March 20th, 1938 and, at the age of four months, travelled to India with my parents. I was a shy, skinny and timid child and my only memories of those early years are full of apprehension, disappointment and fear. My sister, who was born two-and-a-half years after me, looked on life from an entirely opposite point of view. It was not as though I was desperately unhappy. I accepted the way I was as completely normal and although there seemed to be something missing, I could not pin down what it was. I existed rather than lived. God was a word which had no meaning in my early life. What I saw and felt were my reality.

I was extremely jealous of my younger sister's arrival, and this generalised into a dislike of all small babies. Before my sister was born I had been allowed to use her beautifully-prepared cot as a bed for my teddy. Every night I tucked teddy into his bed before climbing into my own, until the day my mother returned with her new baby. Then teddy was turfed out, and I was furious and hurt. Who was this small stranger that usurped my teddy? I tried to put him back in the cot but was told that he would not be safe for the baby. Eventually I was persuaded that he would be much more comfortable in my own bed.

We were brought up by a series of nannies and ayahs – the Indian equivalent of a nanny – as was every other child whose parents were in the Army in India. My parents used to drift in and out of my life either to say good morning or good night. The memories of my mother at that time were of a glamorous, beautiful woman, who wafted in to see us before going out to a dance or social function, leaving the scent she was wearing lingering in the air long after she had gone.

By contrast I remember my father as a rather fierce, strict man. Once he spanked me hard for pulling up an entire flower-bed which had just been planted out. I had been attempting to be helpful by weeding the bed, but an explanation was never asked for. I didn't understand why everyone was so cross and I felt it was grossly unfair. I was also constantly puzzled by the fact that my father always seemed to have one of his arms in plaster. I have since discovered why this was. Being a true

Irishman, he had a passion for horses, particularly those considered unmanageable by others. He took many falls and frequently landed up with a broken collar-bone! For the most part, however, we children lived in a different world from our parents.

India is a place of enormous contrasts. Even as a small child I noticed the difference between the way we lived in our large spacious houses and the way the beggars lived in their rags and tatters, holding up their begging bowls. I couldn't bear to see mules and donkeys with bones sticking out almost through their flesh and hobbled to prevent their moving away, or half-starved dogs scavenging for food. Sometimes, while out on a walk, our ayah took us past the slaughter-house and my whole being revolted at the smell and the sounds coming from that place.

There was one thing I found that released me from all this. When I had paper and pencil in my hand, I became quite oblivious to anything else. I would create my perfect world on paper – the world as I felt it should be. Animals were free, and with four sound legs, everything was beautiful and people had smiling faces. My English nanny would never let me draw for more than half an hour, even though I got such enormous pleasure out of it. I remember having quite a tantrum at the age of three when one of my drawings was taken before I had finished it. Another favourite pastime of mine was to go outside, fill a small bucket with water, mix it with the earth and make models. These were mainly of dogs because they were the creatures that I saw the most.

One morning I woke up early to feel the whole house shaking. Things started to slide across the room and, the next thing I knew, nanny had come in,

scooped up my sister and me and rushed outside into
the garden. What we experienced was, of course,
a minor earth tremor. As a precaution, a tent was
put up during the day and we all slept in this the
following night.

I was a very restless sleeper and would frequently
wake up to find myself at the other end of the
bed, with my bedclothes crumpled up in a heap.
Sometimes in the hot weather, the gardens were
flooded at night so that the parched ground could
get a thorough soaking. Occasionally, our beds were
put outside beyond the veranda in the middle of the
largest flooded lawn. If a party was in progress at the
house, I would lie on my tummy, propping myself up
on my elbows, to watch what was happening in the
dining and drawing rooms. I found this a fascinating
study. My bed became a floating ship on moonlit
waters, and the house some far-off land.

But as soon as I felt drowsy, other emotions
took over, and I felt afraid of the night, imagining
all sorts of weird and terrible shapes, and hearing
sinister rustlings among the trees and bushes. Every
sound became amplified and I lay rigid with fear,
hardly daring to breathe in case any lurking stranger
thought I could see him. My heart thumped as loudly
as a drum, and I longed for morning to come.

When I was five my father was killed while on
manoeuvres, by a shell which accidentally exploded.
I can remember only that he disappeared and never
came back. The matter was never talked about and
I wondered for a long time why he had gone away.
At the time I was puzzled, but then ceased to think
about it. It was not until after I had returned

to England at the age of six or seven, that my grandmother mentioned what had really happened.

I now feel quite strongly that a child should not be shielded from death at whatever age, and however painful. It is an inevitable part of our lives, and facing it is better than cloaking it in silence. Most children are familiar with the death of animals, and show much more resilience when faced with the facts than adults give them credit for. The unknown creates far more apprehension, insecurity and fear in their minds.

My mother married again when I was six. Although I had hardly known my father, I resented my stepfather with my whole being. Soon afterwards my brother was born, and my mother decided to send my sister and me back to England to live with my grandmother.

I think it was probably at this point that I began to wonder why children were born. Were we such a nuisance? It was very confusing and I became unpredictable and more difficult to handle. A nanny was found who was prepared to escort us back by troopship towards the end of the war – the year was 1944. It was a terrible journey – rough and stormy. We also had to contend with tight security and black-outs. Sometimes our life-jackets had to be worn day and night; sleeping in them was extremely uncomfortable. I had never been on board a ship before; I understood little of what was going on and I was afraid.

Christmas Day 1944 was spent at sea. An incident with my nanny at that time remains with me to this day. She had obviously tried very hard to make presents for myself and my sister. Out of scraps

of material, she had secretly managed to make
me a little rag doll, which she presented to me on
Christmas morning before breakfast. The little doll
was sweet, I thought. There was only one problem:
her eyes were far too small. I found a blue pencil and
enlarged them to my own satisfaction. Now the doll
was beautiful. Unfortunately nanny's reaction was
not the same as mine; I was spanked soundly and
the doll was taken away.

That afternoon there was a party with Father
Christmas handing out presents. Imagine my joy
when I was asked if I would like to join him for
tea and found that I need eat only cake! For the first
time in ages life appeared to be sheer bliss. But it
was not to last. As I was eating my first mouthful of
cake, nanny bore down on us. She snatched me up
and said that only bread and butter would do for me
after all the trouble I had caused over the doll which
was now ruined. Life resumed its normal course!
My childhood appears to have been dogged by such
incidents; that nanny, though, was a real dragon and
on arrival at my grandmother's in England she was
immediately asked to leave.

There were many other shocks for my poor grandmother. I was so thin that I was nicknamed the
'Belsen child'. I was a nervous withdrawn little
thing, craving for love, yet unable to give or accept
it: not the kind of child that would be easy to bring
up, or indeed that people would warm to; and my
grandmother, who was the kindest of people, was
nonplussed as to how to cope with me or the situation she now found herself in.

I was six years old, yet I could neither read nor
write. A governess was found to teach me the three

'R's and a painstaking task it was. Letters were simply intriguing shapes, an extension of drawing, but I could see no logic in the order, and I took endless delight in making marvellous patterns out of them. To this day I get them back-to-front and the wrong way round. What fascinated me more was that my grandmother was an artist, and unwittingly she got through to me by showing me how to make colours, how to draw with perspective and many other things. I learned that bread cleaned pictures and egg whites made good glue and glaze, though how she managed that when eggs were rationed I shall never know. Nevertheless I was wary and untrusting, and in the end my grandmother decided to send me away to a boarding school.

This was the first of several schools which, with one exception, I hated. From an assortment of memories, some happy, some sad, one particularly stands out. My bed had some springs missing from it, and one evening our substantially-built matron sat on it and went straight through. I was blamed and made to sleep on a mattress on the music-room floor as a punishment – which I considered very unjust.

However, there were always the holidays. During one of them I discovered to my delight that my grandmother had quite a collection of wonderful old fairy stories, books on animals, and the Beatrix Potter collection. I soaked all these up like blotting paper. My enjoyment was now shared between entering the world of books – I skipped the words I didn't understand – where everything appeared to end happily ever after, and the outdoor world. I loved walking through the woods, or sitting by the small pond beyond them. I watched the tadpoles

wiggling away without a care in the world. I made
gardens out of moss and toadstools. I sat silently
while rabbits scurried past, birds hopped about
looking for food, and cheeky squirrels leapt and
darted from tree to tree – bushy-tailed creatures
which I spent hours drawing.

The gardener, with hatred, declared the rabbits to
be 'varmin' and set gin traps and wire nooses for
them. I used to get into much hot water for untying
the nooses and setting the traps off.

The path down to the woods was flanked with
large rhododendron bushes and, after my grandmother told me that part of *Alice in Wonderland*
had been written in gardens such as these, I wriggled
my way down into the middle of them, letting my
imagination run riot. I felt I knew the exact spot
where Alice had first seen the rabbit. Right inside,
there were special places just like rooms, though
only children were small enough to enter them.

This was my world, a world that did not hurt, a
world that was peaceful and silent – except for the
sounds of animals and birds, the rustling of leaves
in the wind, the crunch of a branch underfoot or
the squelch of mud as my toes disappeared at the
edge of the pond. I wished people did not exist. The
pure beauty of the delicate petals of the primroses
in spring, wild violets, bulrushes, scarlet berries in
winter: these were my joys, and my heart would sing
as I watched, touched, and breathed in the scents of
nature. I wanted to live in this world for ever.

After the holidays, it was school again. I ran
away twice and it was decided to send me to a
different school a little farther away. After discussion with relations a convent was recommended in

Sidmouth, and my sister and I were sent to the Assumption Convent.

I went with a resigned attitude and was surprised at the kindness and consideration shown to us both. There was something intangible about the atmosphere, a caring quality that took me unawares. The chapel was a part of the building, and appeared to be the focal point. It was warm and had a mysterious smell, which I soon discovered was incense. For the first time in my life I felt wrapped in stability and security such as I had not known or experienced before. There was a serenity on the faces of the nuns that reached into my own heart.

I began to feel confident about being 'me'. I also began to relax and catch up academically. I was intrigued by the daily offices in the chapel and enjoyed being a part of them. I bought a little mother-of-pearl rosary, and so began my first efforts at prayer. A nun, catching the expression on my face one day as we were leaving the chapel, took me aside and asked if I would like to spend time there alone while the others were out walking. I said that I would. It was winter and cold outside and my feet were in agony with chilblains, but the chapel was warm, colourful and full of mystery. The veils we wore made us look so angelic! I loved it that each class took it in turn to sing in the choir and although I never understood the Latin, somehow it seemed right. There appeared many feast days, and central to everything was prayer, Christ and the Virgin Mary. If this was Roman Catholicism, then I wanted to be part of it.

I found laughter and happiness. I remember sunny days: lying on the grass in fields and watching the little blue butterflies; picking wild strawberries, putting them in tiny pots and taking them back for tea. We were very near the sea, and in the summer we went down to the beach to swim. I found the sea rather alarming: the waves always seemed big and dangerous; I couldn't swim and was always afraid of going out of my depth. Instead I collected the red clay from the bottom of the cliffs and modelled it into dogs. We always had a fête for the public during the summer term, and I made dozen of dogs and other animals for the stalls.

In the evenings we were read to before going to bed. I loved the stories of Jesus's childhood and listened with rapt attention. The contrast between this and my previous school, where I had been very unhappy, was marked. Much later when I was in real need of help, it was this period of my life that came back to comfort me, having lain dormant and almost forgotten in my subconscious.

For some reason which I never clearly understood my sister and I were taken away from the convent at the ages of seven and nine respectively. I felt like a pawn on a chess board. I cannot remember where my sister was sent at that particular time, but a school in Ascot had been chosen for me, where I stayed for the rest of my schooling. It was divided into junior and senior, both in separate grounds.

I'm not quite sure when my mother and stepfather returned to England, but by this stage there was a wide, almost unbridgeable gap between us, created by my sense of loneliness and of having been deserted; for I felt my mother had begun a new family. By being sent away at the start of their married life, I had a real sense of not truly belonging. My parents were perhaps unaware of this gap but it was very real to me, though I never discussed my feelings with anyone. There seemed no point in doing so for I felt they would not understand.

Soon after their return from India my mother gave birth to a fourth child – a son. At the same time a gradual change was taking place in the relationship between myself and my stepfather. I soon discovered he was the gentlest, kindest of men, strict but fair, showing no favouritism towards his own children. In fact his whole family welcomed us as part of theirs. He treated me very much as a boy, patiently teaching me to cycle, sail, ride, play squash. He was a natural sportsman, with a keen eye for a ball and extremely good at any form of sport. He taught me to play chess and we spent many happy hours battling out a game. He was also a keen reader, and often read aloud to us in the evenings. To me he was someone who could turn life into a romantic adventure. Like my father, he was an Irishman, with a wonderful sense of the ridiculous and no fear. We often did highly irresponsible things together that put my mother into hysterics. We sailed in storms for the fun of it or jumped into swollen rivers; although terrified at times I followed him in sheer trust, confident that he wouldn't ask me to do anything that I was not capable of. Many years later one of my brothers said how much he envied what my stepfather and I had done together, for by the time they grew up he had steadied down considerably.

His family, most of whom lived in Devon, were as kind, generous and full of fun as he – though a more down-to-earth, self-disciplined approach to life than theirs it would be hard to find. Their home in Devon became a haven for me, where life was very different from what I had experienced so far. Horses, dogs, cats, chickens, in fact animals generally, were part and parcel of life.

In the summer months we moved to the lodge on Exmoor and, after packing a few sandwiches, went exploring on horseback through the valleys or over the moor.

My grandmother kept bees, and these too were brought down to give their honey that special taste that comes from heather. I remember days spent ladling honey into jars, getting covered in stickiness up to my elbows in the process.

Most Sundays we walked over the steep hill, through the back of a farm to the little church of Oare nestling by the Doone Valley. Having curled up to read *Lorna Doone* on a few rainy afternoons, my imagination again took over. Consequently, the services made little impression on me. Instead I would be back in time, with scenes from the book alive in front of my eyes.

Those were idyllic days, memorable days; they seemed far removed and apart from the life I mostly led, in which school was a dark, dominant reality.

One incident has stayed in my mind to this day; it was, I believe, a formative one as far as my attitude to tackling life was concerned.

It had been arranged for me to accompany my cousin to a gymkhana a few miles away, an event I was looking forward to immensely. A pony club dance was to follow the gymkhana. I woke up feeling a little unwell but we saddled our ponies and, with our packed lunch, set off together. As the day advanced, I became more and more unwell, and the very thought of riding my pony home was beginning to feel impossible. I shall never know how I got through the day. As we rode back, I was no company for my cousin, who had to keep stopping while I was sick.

On arriving home, I practically fell off my pony, staggered inside and asked if someone could take over from me. I was quite stunned by the reply: 'Animals always come first, whatever the circumstances.' It was a black and white statement and final. I didn't question it, but it was will power alone that took me back to the stables to unsaddle my pony, brush him down, water and feed him. I then collapsed. The doctor was called and I was diagnosed as suffering from water poisoning. I was quite ill for a few days.

This disciplined attitude was one which I adhered to, probably because of my love and respect for the people who taught it to me. With hindsight, however, I can see that an extreme form of this attitude prevented me from 'giving in' and getting help when I needed it at a later date. On the other hand, I think self-discipline and will power helped me through many difficult situations.

Despite the relationship I had with my stepfather, I never discussed my inner thoughts with him or he with me. Emotions were unseemly and kept under tight control. Sex and religion were also taboo subjects. The relationship with my mother, however hard she tried, was always a very distant one, and I look back with sadness on all those wasted years that we could have enjoyed together.

After a few years in England my stepfather was posted to Germany, where we lived for the rest of my schooling. This meant that at half-term and exeats I stayed with a school friend in England. How I envied her her roots, her long-standing friendships, the stability that came from having an established home! I compared this unfavourably with my own comings and goings which, combined with school, were to me a nightmare. I now know that feelings of security have far less to do with moving about than with close-knit family relationships.

I graduated to the senior school eventually where my thinness, combined with my introvert nature, made me a natural target for bullying. Here, there was not a close watch kept on the way we treated each other. Every night I went to bed with a sick feeling in my stomach and an ache in my heart. I hugged the pain to my chest hoping it would go away, but I rarely cried. None of this was at all helpful when it came to studying for exams, and I felt I did badly, getting only four O-levels, Art, Mathematics, English and Religious Knowledge. Art was my mainstay, with the only other pleasure being ballroom dancing – not an academic subject! It was with the greatest relief that, at the age of sixteen, I was allowed to leave school.

Then I was offered the opportunity to become a debutante, but I refused. As I was shy the whole idea filled me with horror, so instead I joined my parents in Malta where my stepfather was posted to serve on Lord Louis Mòuntbatten's staff during the Suez crisis.

My education had not been a good preparation for the society I was about to enter. I was extremely immature, and ill equipped for my later teenage years. I always hung back in a crowd, afraid of being spoken to and not knowing how to answer. Everyone of my age in Malta appeared to me to be very sophisticated and at ease with each other; and, although I longed to join in with the conversation, laughter and larking about that went on, it was as though my feet were rooted to the spot, and I was simply unable to participate. I had no worth in my own eyes, and couldn't imagine why anyone should want to know me.

My reactions in later life to any form of problem or crisis stemmed, I believe, from these years. I always kept my feelings and emotions to myself bottling up anything and everything, regarding the expression of pain, or even joy, as signs of weakness. Fear of exposure caused me to erect barriers which would require much patience, understanding and love to break down.

To many people it must have seemed as though I was brought up in a glamorous setting; to some I probably appeared neither to appreciate nor to be grateful for all my privileges and opportunities. For my part I contemplated the immediate future with a mixture of apprehension and resignation.

# 2

# Blurred Vision

If there were dreams to sell, what would you buy?
Life is a dream to tell, waking, to die.
*Thomas Lovell Beddoes*

I arrived in Malta at 5 a.m. on a hot summer's morning and had barely unpacked my suitcase before a tanned, smiling girl turned up on my doorstep to ask me to join their party for a picnic. I smiled, for her name was Dawn – rather appropriate for that hour of day! They'd be setting off at 9.30 a.m., she said.

This picnic was my first taste of the social set I was about to enter. Everyone was very friendly and articulate. I envied them their social grace. Nonetheless I enjoyed the casual atmosphere and ready laughter, although their beautifully-shaped brown bodies, glistening with water in the sunshine as they dived off the rocks into the sea, showed up my thinness and very white skin – the latter an obvious indication that I had only just arrived. What bowled me over were their genuine efforts to make friends with me and eventually I became an accepted part of 'the set'. We met all the right people, were seen at all the right places and invited to all the important balls and occasions. Every Sunday we converged on someone's launch and sped out to a deserted bay to swim, aquaplane and generally laze about. It all seemed a little unreal and too glamorous to be true.

It was at this time that I was introduced to 'table turning' as it was called. I was quite fascinated by the speed with which the glass could move around a table without any apparent physical help from anyone. We put Scrabble letters in a circle round the glass and asked it a variety of ridiculous questions. We never became serious and treated the whole thing as a joke. But I felt we were unaware of hidden depths in our subconscious minds and of a power beyond our understanding. I felt slightly uneasy about what we were doing. Many years later, I was completely taken aback at the strongly adverse reaction of a friend on hearing about all this. I then began to appreciate that, however innocent our fun had appeared to be, it could have opened doors to an inner darkness over which we have no control.

It wasn't long before I became very restless. I needed to earn some money to keep up with the activities of our crowd and felt that I couldn't justify continually asking my parents to subsidise my pleasures. So another girl and I answered an advertisement for teachers in a Maltese school. We were both accepted, though neither of us had had any formal teacher training. I found the job an immense challenge. Having recently left school, the role reversal was an eye-opener.

I soon discovered that I had one of the naughtiest girls in the school in my class. She was nine years old and couldn't read. Because I had suffered as a child with reading difficulties, I was determined to make things better for her and to find the time to teach her on an individual basis. This proved easier than expected: she was often sent out of classes for being disruptive. Although it meant extra marking and preparation of class work had therefore to be done at home, I grabbed this tousled-headed child each time I found her the wrong side of the door and gave her individual lessons such as I had been given as a child.

At first she couldn't believe that she was having to work, then she showed astonishment that someone cared, after which she sat down to learn in earnest. Together we won through and, after several months of exhausting work, and at times, frustration, she was able to read. For me it was an exhilarating experience – a shared achievement. More significantly, though I didn't realise this at the time, I had formed a relationship in which my purpose was to benefit the other person.

The transformation in this girl's attitude to school was remarkable. No longer did she try to hide her inability to cope under the guise of naughtiness. I shall never forget her hug in my last term as she whispered in my ear, 'I love you Miss Sudden!' She never could pronounce my maiden name, Sugden. She had touched my heart in a way no other person ever had.

As far as my social life was concerned, the change from being rather solitary to being part of a glamorous set played havoc with my bottled-up emotions. My feelings were intense. I found it very difficult to have a light-hearted relationship with a boy, and would often imagine myself 'in love'. When the boy moved away, as so often happened, I would be broken-hearted.

I could also be incredibly stubborn. I was invited to a ball on my current boy-friend's last evening in Malta before he sailed. I had not been feeling well all day and as the evening approached the most terrible pains shot through my stomach. I gritted my teeth and dressed for the ball. The door-bell rang. I just managed to answer it before dropping to the floor in a heap. I was rushed into hospital and operated on for acute appendicitis. Two operations and a few weeks later, I was home, but feeling as weak as a kitten.

It was while convalescing at home that I had a strange – and to me at the time – inexplicable experience. It was something that was to recur, including on the night of my husband's death.

I had been allowed out of hospital on the condition that I spent a considerable time resting, for I was still very weak, had a drainage tube in my side, and needed a daily visit from our doctor.

One morning I woke up early. The sun was streaming into my bedroom, for I always opened my curtains at night before getting into bed. My whole body felt fuzzy, as though I had pins and needles. I seemed to be two people: one in bed and the other floating above it looking down at myself. I had no control over my body's movement, yet I was somehow free. I saw with remarkable clarity but passively, as an observer. It took an enormous amount of effort for me to integrate into being one person again lying on the bed. The whole experience had a dream-like quality, but I knew it had been no dream. I was unable to discuss this phenomenon with anyone, fearing that people would laugh at me.

It was in Malta that I met my first husband. He was older than me, incredibly good-looking and worldly. I was bowled over by his attentions, and at seventeen imagined myself to be madly in love with him.

I hadn't much experience with men, and looking back cannot imagine why such an apparently sophisticated man would have wanted to marry me. We were very different, for I was socially shy and gauche. Maybe we both had needs that I was too immature to understand properly. He too was a soldier, and there is no doubt that his dress-uniform, particularly in such a glamorous social setting, added to the attraction.

My parents, though not forbidding our engagement, were disturbed, and begged me to wait till I was a little older. At seventeen I thought I knew it all, and refused to listen to their advice. But I did have a sense of foreboding that things were not as they should be, though I was too shy to talk this out with my fiancé. There were several occasions when I tried to mention my fears but as our wedding day drew nearer, my courage weakened and finally failed.

I couldn't cope with the thought of my parents cancelling all the arrangements and sending back all the presents. I realise this only highlights the immaturity of our relationship.

We were married in Tisbury church, Wiltshire, when I was twenty. We had a week's honeymoon in Jersey before he went back to Germany on army manoeuvres, and I returned to my parents' house in Wiltshire. It was not a good way to start a marriage. Eventually a quarter became available in Germany, and I flew over to begin a new life.

Things went wrong almost immediately. I was terribly shy; he did not realise how much I needed his support, particularly at social functions – and outside working hours, Army life was a round of parties and entertainment of various kinds.

He adored horses, and was an extremely good rider. He often left me for hours on end in a room full of strangers while he went off to check on his horses, particularly before a big show-jumping event. I found this unnerving and difficult to cope with.

I had never learned properly how to give or receive love, and I was very naïve. None of this can have been easy for him but, since we were both used to hiding our emotions, we were never able to bring ourselves to talk through these really important issues. It was a recipe for disaster sooner or later. Into this rather tense environment my first two children, Richard and Michael, were born.

However many distractions I sought, in the shape of social work, sport, voluntary work and so on, I continued to seek that elusive spiritual something which I knew was missing but which I could not explain. Sadly I did not know where to begin, having neither the right guide-lines nor the relevant experience.

Although my husband and I stayed together – initially for the sake of appearances, and ultimately for that of the children – it was not long before we were both living a lie. In the end we had to acknowledge to each other that our relationship had no future. We had both been brought up to think divorce was wrong, and I found the disgrace of failure very difficult to come to terms with.

I have spoken to endless people since about the rights and wrongs of divorce. There is no easy answer. Some have stayed together through thick and thin for the children's sake, but have become bitter, living separate, isolated lives so that the children miss out on love and joy – their essential nourishment. Others have managed to come through by maintaining a kind of truce. Still others have parted company, believing their children would be less traumatised that way.

Whichever way one chooses, the children are always caught in the middle, carrying around with them unnecessary guilt, blaming themselves for their parents' unhappiness. Though not at fault, they cannot help but be affected by an atmosphere in which heartache, a sense of failure, feelings of guilt and disillusionment, are making their presence felt.

Looking back, I have often wondered whether, with a Christian commitment and attitude and the resource of God's love, things might have been different. I like to think so, while knowing that even with all that, failures do occur, such is our human frailty.

The divorce went through and soon afterwards we both remarried. For me it would have been wiser to have waited, allowing time for reflection and for hurts to heal. But I felt I had been given a second chance.

Our new home was full of laughter and I became more confident as a person. I also began to take more interest in the children whom I felt I had let down badly through my preoccupation with my own misery. I had 'fed and watered' them, but given them nothing of myself, but happiness and a sense of security enabled me to recognise this.

My second husband, Christopher, an Irishman like my father and stepfather, was also in the Army. He had a similar sense of the ridiculous and of fun, as well as courage, and the 'gift of the gab'. It had been his resemblance to my stepfather that had drawn me to him. We found joy together in the simplest things. After we had our own two children, Charlie and Victoria, I was content to see Christopher and the older two enjoying themselves in the same way as my stepfather and I had done. Our family had become a unit, whole in itself, releasing me from the strain of living a falsehood. Being part of this precious whole was all I wanted from life.

Although a Catholic, Christopher agreed that Charlie and Victoria should be christened in the Church of England, so that there would be no distinction between them and Richard and Michael. My last child being a girl made my happiness complete.

Soon after Charlie was born we were stationed in Germany which was now becoming quite familiar territory. We chose to live fifteen miles outside the Army camp, both of us agreeing that we needed the space and freedom away from the protocol and restrictions of Army life.

The only jarring note occurred when I had a miscarriage before the birth of our youngest child. Christopher was on exercise at the time, the two elder children were at school in England and I was alone with our one-year-old in our rather isolated villa. When I realised what had happened – a very frightening experience for me on my own – I scooped up Charlie and drove the fifteen miles into the camp surgery. My son was immediately taken off my hands and an ambulance called. Suddenly I remembered our rabbits and insisted that I should return and make arrangements for their well-being. Apart from physical restraint, there was nothing anyone could have done to dissuade me, and I drove back to our local farm, where I proceeded in halting German to explain my situation to Herr Zander, the farmer. Dumbfounded with astonishment, he agreed to take care of the rabbits until my return. I arrived back in the camp to find the ambulance still waiting. I felt ridiculous, but relieved as we drove into Rinteln, the nearest military hospital, where I spent the next three days.

This kind of behaviour was typical of me. I would carry something through no matter what it cost me, for I had taken to heart the lesson learned earlier about the importance of seeing to the needs of our animals. Also, the ability to take physical and emotional endurance to its limits had become a habit which by this time I was unable to break.

Soon afterwards, Christopher decided he would like to return to England and start a new life based on being a family together, without all the separations that commitment to the Army required. We moved back into our little cottage which he had bought eighteen months earlier; and my longings to be settled in our own home began at last to be fulfilled.

The simplest things gave me pleasure: cooking a meal with our own saucepans; making our own curtains; putting up kitchen cupboards and knowing they were there to stay; sleeping in our own bed and waking up to familiar surroundings; knowing that I could plant a tree and watch it grow; giving the children a real home of their own to grow up in. My dog, left behind in England while we'd been in Germany, returned to live with us and we were able to go for wonderful walks once more over the Downs. The intensity of my joy was so great that I could hardly contain it, and sometimes I would stand in the garden and just gaze out at our little patch of paradise. I felt I had been given everything and I ceased to search for that missing spiritual element. Not once did the idea of entering our church, or joining in with the activities of our church community, ever enter my mind.

The children blossomed within this environment of happiness. When my daughter was four months old, we decided to have both our children christened together. The ceremony took place in the little church which lay at the bottom of my parents' garden. My grandmother, overjoyed to see the baptisms of her fifth and sixth great-grandchildren, sat in quiet splendour throughout the family ceremony.

She was not to live much longer. I knew this, but still found it hard to accept. It had seemed that she had always been and would always be there, indestructible. My father's death hadn't seemed very real to me and I had been abroad when my other grandmother had died.

I was rung up one afternoon from the home for the elderly, where she then lived, and told that my grandmother had had an attack and had only a few hours to live. No other members of our family could be contacted, for they were all out, so I was asked to come at once. Having put Victoria in her carry-cot, and Charlie and the dog in the back of the car, I drove over as quickly as possible.

It was a terrible shock to see my grandmother looking so grey and weak. Her breathing was shallow and I had to lean close to listen to her feeble voice. I felt helpless as she called over and over again for her daughter, since I had no idea where my mother was. I stayed with her, holding her hand and sponging her forehead gently, trying to soothe her anxieties. Most of the afternoon was spent between being with Granny and quietening the children downstairs. In my urgency to come, I had forgotten to bring a bottle of milk for Victoria who became very hungry. In the end, the nurses said that my grandmother would probably last for several more hours and suggested that I should go home and feed my baby. I left reluctantly and on arriving home heard the phone ringing.

It was the home for the elderly to say that my grandmother had just died. I looked at the young child secure in my arms, with her life just beginning, contrasting this with an old lady dying alone. How I wish I had not left her! In the years that followed I had nightmares about this, and carried a terrible feeling of guilt about letting her down. My only consolation was that over the years we had grown very close and that, since our return to England, she had spent many happy days simply being with us, delighting in having her grandchildren and great-grandchildren around her. She had always been a great chatterbox, but listening to her had been like opening up the pages of an exciting, living history book. Almost blind, she had no longer been able to use her artist's skills with the brush, but she had painted history for us with colourful words instead.

I found it difficult to communicate how I felt about her to Christopher and was sad that he didn't seem to understand my grief, although several years earlier he had lost his father.

As in all marriages, ours had its stresses and tensions, but on the whole we were able to talk them out together. It seemed to me as though Christopher had given me everything; I therefore put him on a pedestal. I felt as though I had been saved. Life seemed to sparkle with freshness and gaiety. Not that there weren't any difficulties. One of these was Christopher's asthma, brought on by household dust or hay-fever. Twice I had to rush him into hospital, wondering whether I would make it in time. My youngest son's delicate constitution was another worry, and I wondered if he would ever become strong like other children. But apart from worries like these, I was very happy.

It was in this our first home that I discovered the miracle of growing plants from cuttings. I've always had an affinity with wild life. As a child I had been drawn to nature as a means of healing the hurt and confusion I so often felt. My ability to be still for long periods of time meant that wild creatures, such as rabbits and birds, foxes and mice, would venture very close to me. Theirs was a freedom I envied. I could not, and still cannot, bear to see any wild animal caged.

If I found a mouse indoors, instead of chasing it out, I often simply stood still and watched it.

It was enchanting to see the agility with which it moved about. My mother sometimes reminded me of one particular afternoon when, on opening the study door, to her horror she found me sitting on the floor with an inquisitive little mouse playing in the folds of my skirt.

I think I also have a gift in my hands which animals have sensed. Once, in Germany, the local children brought me a very mangled leveret. It had been badly mauled by a dog. I dried it and held it gently, willing the poor little thing to live. For the next few days, I'm sure it was this loving will power that kept it alive. Later it gave us all an immense amount of pleasure as it bounced round the house and furniture, growing bigger, stronger and cheekier by the day.

I have often held sick birds and rabbits, and noticed how they have perked up afterwards. Body warmth and security, I believe, had much to do with this; at any rate, for whatever reason, animals appear to have no fear when I am holding them. I'm sure it was an outpouring of love that kept my dog alive for his last year. Only after he had been put down and I could relax, did I realise how much of myself had been drained in keeping him going.

Looking back, I believe that almost without realising it, I was engaging in a kind of prayer. Once, when a friend's child was in a coma in hospital after a serious riding accident, I found myself willing this same current of love to her with great intensity in the hope that she would be healed. Afterwards I was quite drained, but the next day I heard that the child had unexpectedly come out of her coma.

I'm sure that many people have the gift of healing, to a greater or lesser extent, without even realising it. I was told that a distant relative of ours had dedicated her life to using the healing powers in her hands for the good of others. More frequently, people use their gifts through medicine, the veterinary service and other recognised methods of healing.

Changes occurred in our lives when Christopher decided to set up his own business instead of working for other people. This entailed moving, which I found very hard indeed. Our first house together had been so special. I had grown to love its character and had made many friends in the area. Nevertheless, being together as a family was of greater importance.

Our new home was spacious, but the house and garden needed a lot of work. This was a challenge. We lived next to a farm. One hot summer's day, during a time of drought when the ground was brick-hard, I was attempting to dig out and create a rose-bed by the house. As I worked, making very little impression in the earth, I sensed that a figure was watching me. Looking up, I saw my neighbour, grinning and leaning against a dry-stone wall. My futile but determined efforts to turn a field into a garden obviously amused him. This was the beginning of a very good relationship.

Many people felt we were in an isolated position, but I enjoyed that. Nature surrounded us, yet we were not often alone for very long. Having a large house meant that we could have people to stay more easily, and there were precious few weeks when there were no visitors or house-guests.

Because so many people called or stayed and I was busy looking after four children, I rarely ventured into our local village, so I never met the community. It was my loss, although I was oblivious of it at the time. I adored gardening, and spent my summer days planning and planting a variety of flowers and vegetables. Clematis, wisteria, roses and jasmine were trained up the walls of the house. I wanted their scents to pervade and their colours to spill out everywhere. I wanted the barren, wind-swept field surrounding the house to be filled with trees, bushes, flowers, and a vegetable garden. When a hedgerow was pulled out near by, I dragged some of it home and planted it. The ground was so rocky that it used to take me about two hours to dig a hole deep enough to plant a tree, but I persevered.

I often walked with our dog in the morning before breakfast so that I could catch a glimpse of the early sun on the crops or the dew on the cobwebs over the wild roses. In winter, I took many photos of the sun rising over the snow. Every season brought its own magic. If there had not been time before breakfast, I walked after the children had gone to school, entering into the joy of the skylark's song, the beauty of the yellow-hammer flying over the hedges or of a fox slipping through the undergrowth. Sometimes I simply stopped and gazed at the clouds as a storm gathered, or downed tools in the evening to watch a sunset. All this wealth, it seemed to me, came through Christopher.

For three years I worked on the house and garden, seeing it gradually take shape, while Christopher put his own business of chartered surveying on its feet. They were probably the happiest years of my life.

We entertained frequently, and the manual work of the day was balanced by relaxed conversations in the evening.

Then I went into a private hospital in London for a hysterectomy. Everything was arranged very quickly and I only just managed to organise matters for the children and Christopher in my absence. It was probably as well that I did not have much time to think or worry, as I become apprehensive at the very mention of hospitals.

A few days after the operation I experienced once again something akin to what had occurred in Malta years before. I woke up in great pain and reached out to press the bell. I found I couldn't move my hand. Instead I seemed to be looking down at my inert body on the bed with the same sensations as before; those of floating and pins and needles. This time I felt frightened and tried calling for help, but could make no noise. I had a great sense of urgency about integrating with my body, so every ounce of will went into my efforts to do this. I succeeded in the end. Really terrified by this time, I not only rang the bell but also managed to reach and open the door before collapsing. A night nurse who was outside another patient's room came and scooped me up into her arms. She took me back to bed and I was attended to. The next day I was told that a secondary infection had set in. My stay in hospital was a little longer than I had anticipated.

Afterwards, it was wonderful to be home again, although I had not bargained for the frustrations of taking life easy. I had always kept active with tennis, squash, riding, gardening and walking, and found the whole idea of gentle exercise intolerable. One day I sneaked into the vegetable garden to plant my onion sets, hoping Christopher wouldn't find out!

I still had the pleasure of taking my dog for gentle walks, but he became very ill and in the end had to be put down. He had also gone blind and seeing him in pain was unbearable.

I tried to make his last day as happy as possible. The weather was perfect and we went for a final walk together through the fields. The vet had agreed to come to our house and was waiting for us when we returned. Max lay with his head resting in my arms in the garden, wagging his tail as I talked to him gently. The pain inside me was terrible.

We buried him in the garden. I found a large stone from an ancient chapel which had stood in a neighbouring field. We built a curved step over his grave between two flower beds, and incorporated the chapel stone. In this setting I felt he could rest in peace for ever.

After this blow and still frustrated by my limitations, I decided to pluck up courage and ask a near by clay pigeon coach if he would teach me how to shoot. I felt this might compensate for my lack of other sporting activities. I always remember arriving for my first session, feeling extremely foolish, conscious that I was a woman about to embark on what was predominantly a man's sport. I was faced with two men, one of whom I discovered, was a national coach. This nearly made me turn tail and run. How very different my story would have been if I had!

This was an opening into a new world. I soon discovered that, despite various disadvantages, I was a natural shot. It was not long before I was working on a shooting ground to earn enough money to pay for my lessons. At my first competition, my stomach was full of butterflies, but from then onwards I went from strength to strength. I learned how to shoot, to lay out and run competitions and to referee. I travelled and experienced every kind of discipline. I was involved in discussions on courses and coaching, and eventually qualified as a coach myself. I worked long hours on freezing cold days and late into summer evenings, familiarising myself with every aspect of this sport, with a view to being able eventually to turn it into a lucrative business.

Meanwhile, Christopher had taken up mountaineering as a relaxation from his business life.

# 3

# Breaking Point

O the mind, mind has mountains: cliffs of fall
Frightful, sheer, no-man-fathomed.

*G.M. Hopkins*

I cannot say precisely when things started to go
wrong in our marriage. I only know that what
we did was indicative of our inner feelings and
realities. Christopher began to live for the next
mountaineering expedition. In many ways I can
understand why he loved climbing. Not only was
the pull and challenge of the mountains very strong,
but he actually felt better at high altitudes: his hay
fever and asthma disappeared and he was able to
breathe properly. At home in Wiltshire, injections,
masks and inhalers never completely alleviated his
breathing difficulties.

Perhaps I had begun to realise that we were in
financial difficulties because of Christopher's mountaineering. He made light of the cost of expeditions.
I discovered afterwards that he had cashed in all
pension funds for our future as well as building up
a huge overdraft to pay for his hobby, which had
grown into an obsession. He tried to persuade me

that his climbing cost nothing, but the tension in his face betrayed him.

It was not, however, his love for mountains that I found the most disturbing; and without question his climbing friends were open, honest people, who looked life full in the face with courage, and I was at ease in their company.

What troubled me more was the strange possessive relationship which was growing up between Christopher and another man. I did not know then, any more than I know now, the nature of their relationship, but it was unlike the relationships we had with all our other friends, in that I felt completely excluded. The full impact of this relationship hit me the night before Christopher was due to go on a British expedition to Alaska, and I had the first frightening glimpse of something deeply amiss.

It had all been very exciting. Much of the administration had been done around our kitchen table. Everyone was aware that several other expeditions had failed with tragic results, but the positive enthusiasm produced an optimism that spread throughout the team.

As they were probably going to be away for about a month, depending on the weather conditions in Alaska, I wanted to make Christopher's last evening at home a very special family occasion. We arranged to have an early supper so that the children could join in. We usually ate later in the evening after they had gone to bed.

We had great fun planning what we would eat and do. It was a wonderful sunny afternoon, and after collecting Victoria from school, she and I took the dogs – both bred from Max – for a walk in the woods, singing as we went. Suddenly I felt that all was right with the world, that my earlier fears were unfounded and that I was very happy and proud of what my husband was about to attempt.

We returned from our walk, collected Charlie from school, cooked Christopher's favourite meal and waited. We waited and waited. He didn't come home. The children became fractious and hungry, and I felt sick in the pit of my stomach.

At 9 p.m. a car drove down the drive. It was Jonathan, whose relationship with Christopher I had found so difficult to understand. Christopher was with him in the car. They had both been drinking and said they were late because Christopher's car had broken down.

With relief that Christopher was safe I turned my attention to the matter of rescuing his car. I suggested ringing the AA, but the two men were reluctant to do so. On pursuing the matter, and heading for the telephone, Christopher stopped me. 'You fool!' he said. 'There is nothing wrong with the car: it was just an excuse so that Jonathan could take me to the station in the morning. The car is at his house.'

I saw then what I had not seen before, that Jonathan was beginning to mean more to Christopher than us – his family. Something had gone very wrong, but I still couldn't quite pinpoint what it was.

As he burst out with the truth, I thought I was going to die, and I hardly noticed as Jonathan slunk out of the house and quietly drove away. The children were by this time too tired to eat, and I felt too sick. In a daze I put them to bed and told them to be good. I then told Christopher to get into my car, so that we could collect his and bring it home. Strangely enough I never blamed him, but my heart turned cold with anger against Jonathan. Never had I felt such hatred for another human being. It was the most destructive, violent emotion I have ever experienced. The fact that I was dealing with a relationship outside my own experience made me feel quite helpless, as I struggled with pain and anger together. I shall never know what appealed to Christopher in this man; perhaps it was the lack of commitment and responsibilities which such a friendship seemed to offer. I do know that it put an unbearable strain on our marriage.

We hardly spoke that evening, and the next morning I quietly drove Christopher to the station. I helped him into the train with all his climbing gear. As the train drew out of the station, tears streamed down my face. Would I see him again? If he came back at all would he be coming back to us or to Jonathan?

While he was away I learned that things had also begun to go wrong in the office, and I realised too, that he was beginning to drink more than usual. His attitude, it seemed to me, had become unbalanced; his work and family had ceased to matter.

The expedition was not successful, but everyone returned safely. Christopher seemed subdued and, when I plucked up courage to talk about this, he promised to end his relationship with Jonathan. For a while he did, and we became a family again. I put the matter out of my mind.

Several months later, however, Christopher started coming in late in the evenings, often missing supper altogether. It didn't take me long to find out where he was spending his evenings. Weighed down by the emotional tensions of the situation and the worry of accumulating debts, he began to drink more heavily. Our children's book of chess disappeared, and I found that Christopher had taken this over to Jonathan's house where he was now playing chess and doing other things that he had previously done at home with us. I discovered, too, that he was turning to Jonathan to discuss family matters, and even making decisions over the children's schooling, as though their future was no longer my concern.

In the last three months of his life, Christopher underwent a personality change. His behaviour became unpredictable: one minute he would be completely charming, the next aggressive and violent. He began to have delusions of grandeur. A fit man himself, he started to despise those that were not, including his own son Charlie who, through no fault of his own, was at that time physically weak. This aggravated Christopher beyond measure. At times I was frightened for the children and for myself.

Nor was Christopher the only one who had changed. I was not the quiet unassuming person I had been. My confidence in myself, through marriage to Christopher, had grown. I knew now that I was capable of living life in my own right, outside family commitments. My abilities in clay pigeon shooting had also boosted my self-image. Christopher could not accept the change in me and became jealous of my success.

For months I agonised about what to do. In the
competitive world of clay shooting, I was being
given opportunities beyond my wildest dreams.
Should I give them all up? As Christopher spent
more and more time away from us, I shouldered
the responsibilities that we had previously shared.
Reason told me that giving time to the family,
running a large house, working a full week on
the shooting ground and competing at weekends
was too big a burden for one person. So, early in
December, I decided to give up everything to do
with clay shooting. It was a very painful decision
but I thought it might help our marital situation.

It didn't. Things went from bad to worse. Our
financial situation became more critical. With the
two youngest children in private schools, we could
not afford the climbing expeditions that Christopher
was now embarking upon. But he continued to
ignore the problems facing us.

Although we didn't fully realise this at the time,
we were near 'overload' as far as stress was concerned. One day much later, I was to watch what
happens when a computer disk is overloaded. Before my astonished eyes, the machine seemed to
go berserk. Each letter was still present but in such
a jumbled-up form as to be rubbish. I realise that
something similar can happen with human beings
when we go over the safety limit.

People tell me that I am a practical, sensible
sort of person, someone who thinks before acting.
My grandmother always referred to me as steady
and reliable. But in my secret self I know I am
sensitive, a dreamer and a romantic. This inner
self rarely showed: I had trained myself never

to show my emotions – never to cry in public, never to raise my voice in argument unnecessarily. Because I tended to get on with the job in hand without making a fuss, I gave the impression of being competent and confident. I rather scorned people who said they couldn't do a thing simply because they had never tried it before. I remember once being presented with a dead pheasant. As I was looking at this with some horror and wondering how I was going to deal with it, the person who had given me the bird said briskly, 'My dear child, have you no idea how to pluck it?' The next thing I knew I was being whisked into an enormous kitchen where I was told exactly what to do and expected to do it. I emerged triumphant sometime later, with a rather mangled offering for supper!

Underneath the façade of coping well, I was in a state of great inner distress. Strangers or even friends might not have noticed this, and I even tried to fool myself about the way things were.

Back in October I had noticed that my competition results were beginning to drop. Practice had failed to improve things because, though I had not realised this, stress was the underlying cause. I was having difficulty trying to be logical or to concentrate for any length of time: after reading a page or two of a book, I found myself gazing blankly into space. At night, utterly exhausted, I fell asleep as soon as my head hit the pillow, but woke up an hour or two later and tossed and turned for most of the night. I often had terrible nightmares and by the morning felt completely drained. Having always been a good sleeper, this pattern was out of character. I felt permanently sick in the pit of my stomach, unable to think of anything except my inner pain. Feelings of detachment and panic were not uncommon. It was particularly terrifying that I often blanked out while driving.

I cared for the children on 'automatic pilot'. It felt as though there was a great distance between myself and the rest of the world. When I was forced back to reality, the pain was so intense that I could hardly bear it. Dimly, I was aware that I needed some kind of help but was not sure what. Besides, there were other things to attend to. Buying Victoria a pair of shoes and other small tasks became issues of enormous importance. It was as though my life depended on clinging on to the small things; doing them seemed more important than seeing my doctor.

Struggling to stay on an even keel was made more difficult by the fact that Christopher was finding fault with everything I did. I was being slowly hammered into the ground as in desperation I continued to clutch at the day-to-day administration to keep me going.

Christmas came, but there was no joy in it for us. Strangely enough, the one person to whom I felt I could turn to for help, was Christopher's mother. But Christopher said he didn't want anyone, even his mother, staying with us over Christmas. I found this surprising and odd. I couldn't remember a Christmas without some member of his family celebrating with us. I did write a letter to my mother-in-law, but although desperate and longing to confide in her, I did not have the courage to express this on paper. I felt, then, as though my last hope had gone.

Christopher's fortieth birthday fell on 29th December. I had arranged a special party for him. It is one memory that stays. I can even see the food laid out on the dining-room table. He approached his birthday with a mixture of feelings, for he had always been concerned about growing old and unfit. Although I used to laugh with him about this, I knew his fear was quite genuine. Because of this fear, I think he developed a disregard for danger. He said that he would prefer to fall down a crevasse rather than grow old.

The party was enjoyed by the guests, I hope, but not by me. Christopher had been edgy all day, and during the evening, leaning against the mantelpiece and laughing, he said that he would not live beyond forty. I was horrified by his words and hastily left the room to busy myself with something or other. Life without Christopher seemed intolerable, unthinkable.

But a few days later, the bomb exploded. Christopher announced that he would be leaving us. As if this wasn't devastating enough, he added that he would be putting our house on the market and buying something for himself, next door to his friend, Jonathan.

My world had fallen apart.

The events of the last few days of Christopher's life are a hazy, disjointed memory, with some areas a complete blank. The only things that I can remember clearly were that I still hadn't bought Victoria's shoes and that I must see my doctor. I suspect that my mind was desperately avoiding the real issues at stake.

I also remember that we had friends round for drinks and a business discussion on our last evening together, and that I couldn't find the sherry. I cannot recall Christopher's actual words, but he was angry and made me look very stupid. It was at this moment that the strain reached breaking point, and I lost touch with reality – something that can happen to anyone who is under great physical or emotional stress. I became completely detached from my body, and experienced again the strange sensation of floating above myself. It was the only time this had ever happened in the presence of other people. I seemed to be above my chair, looking down on everyone – a passive observer, yet still a member of the group. I could not feel anything, although I saw myself touch chairs, doors, glasses. Time ceased to exist for me and the events that followed have been pieced together from conversations with the police, psychiatrists and my solicitor.

Our friends having gone, the children were watching television. Christopher had left the room to do something in his study which was at the top of the stairs and led into our bedroom. A large chest of drawers stood outside the study door. Charlie and I had been rabbit shooting earlier in the afternoon. Our guns were propped up against the chest and waiting to be cleaned. I kept the cleaning equipment and cartridges in one of the top drawers of the chest. Ironically, leaflets containing the safety rules and regulations of our clay-shooting club were lying on top of the chest.

I went up to see Christopher. From this moment, events became a blur and I will never know for sure exactly what took place. I thought I saw Christopher coming towards me with his arms wide open. Yet I also saw hatred in his eyes. It was the most terrible shock when later I was made to look at police photographs and realised that he had not been walking towards me. I never heard the shot and neither did the children.

Disjointed memories are all that I have of what followed. Screaming for help. Friends trying to dial my solicitor's number, which I was incapable of finding. Sitting on the playroom floor, turning a couple of ribbed objects over and over in my jeans' pocket – the almost automatic, repetitious movement seemingly soothing. After a time I took them out and looked at them curiously: two brown cartridges, one live and the other used. I handed them over to the police. I felt very cold. People came and went. I think I said to the children, 'I've done something terrible.' I was not allowed to go upstairs to see Christopher. Friends came and took the children away. I have no memory at all of their reaction.

I was taken to Chippenham Police Station, I discovered afterwards, although I have no recollection of the journey there. I was vaguely aware of my solicitor and the police and of having to make a statement. I was absolutely exhausted, and the process appeared to take hours. I think someone was a little cross because I was so slow in answering questions. I tried to sign the pages, but my hands felt like lead weights. I fought desperately to remain conscious. People's voices sounded distorted, reminding me

of the old-fashioned gramophone running down in
my grandmother's home. My movements seemed
strange and slow, like a nightmare in which we try
and run away from something terrible but can only
move at half speed. It was an extreme effort to do
or say anything. I felt I was fighting for my sanity.
Everything was dark.

I was put in a room with bars. There was a bench
with a blanket on it, otherwise the place was bare,
I think. I couldn't understand why my shoes, laces,
hair-band and watch were removed. I think I drifted
in and out of consciousness. The bars of my cage –
as I thought of it – seemed to be set at an odd angle.
I had difficulty in breathing and strange noises were
coming from my throat. People kept standing over
me saying things which I couldn't grasp.

Sometime, presumably the next day, I was taken
to a surgery to see a doctor. His face was so ex-
pressionless, that as I was stripped and examined,
I imagined myself not as a person, but as a carcass
of beef in a butcher's cold store, waiting to be hung
up on a meat-hook with the rest after inspection.

Every article of clothing that I had on was put
into plastic bags and taken away, and I was led to
a chair, where I sat naked except for a white gown,
for what seemed like hours while arrangements were
made for someone to return to our house and collect
fresh clothing for me to put on.

I don't know how my eldest son, Richard, discovered what had happened, but at one point I found
myself in his arms. I noticed that he couldn't stop
shaking. I recognised my own doctor who came
to see me, and for whom evidently I had been
calling. He sat across the table from me and took

my hands, but I was beyond speech, and could only look at him.

From the moment I had shot my husband to the moment I arrived in Pucklechurch, it was as though the light had gone for ever, for I can only remember one long terrible darkness. I felt I had sunk to the bottom of the pit. I was sure I had entered hell.

# 4

## Prison on Remand

There is no pit so deep that he is not deeper.
*Corrie Ten Boom*

I was driven, as I realised later, to Pucklechurch
Remand Centre. I was so tired it didn't matter that
I was handcuffed between two policewomen. It felt
good to be sitting by another human being. All I
wanted to do was to sleep. Laying my head on
the shoulder of one of the women, I heard her
companion murmur something like, 'Poor thing,
she's falling asleep,' as I sank into oblivion.

At the remand centre, I let myself be stripped,
weighed and inspected. There was a terrible struggle
to remove my wedding ring; by the time it had
been successfully removed, my finger was bruised,
swollen and painful. I remember apologising for
being fat, but my voice sounded a long way off.
My body didn't feel as though it belonged to me. I
remember being put in a warm bath. Then someone
was washing my hair, speaking quietly and gently,
as though any harsh noise might send me berserk.
I was put into a white garment which tied at the
back, and told not to be afraid: what was happening

was only for my own good. I didn't fully understand
what was going on. Then I was taken to a cell with
a mattress on the floor covered with some kind of
heavy blanket. Apart from a single light bulb over-
head, the room was bare. Afterwards I learned that
I had been put in 'strip conditions' in the hospital
wing to prevent my committing suicide. Later one
of the nurses – someone with a heart – returned with
my ring which she put back on, telling me to keep
quiet about it. She also brought me some tablets. I
swallowed them, not knowing what they were.

I seemed to be surrounded by swirling blackness,
vague and confused questions churning round in my
mind. Was I in hell? Was I insane? I lay inert, not
able to move, drifting from semi-consciousness to
consciousness and back again. I lost all sense of
time. What had happened to the daylight? Scenes
floated into my mind and then receded: my eldest son Richard holding me in his arms at the
police station, and shaking with shock; my doctor
reaching out to hold my hands across a table; my
hand trying to sign the statement that I didn't
understand. My mind moved back and forth in
waves, with no logical sequence. At one moment,
I seemed to be caught up in a blazing fire, from
which Christopher was reaching down to rescue
me. At the next, I was spiralling down into a
whirlpool, to the very depths of darkness where
nothing existed.

With curiosity, I viewed my hands. Why hadn't
someone cut them off? They were evil. They did not
belong to me. As I looked at them, they appeared to
be oozing a black substance. I was afraid to touch
anything for fear of contaminating it.

In the next few days people came and went. Friends and family came to see me. Sometimes I recognised them, sometimes I didn't. It must have been terrible for them. Eventually I was given a proper cell, with a bed and blankets, but there was a crack in the window through which the wind whistled. It was very cold. I wore all my clothes, including my anorak, to try and keep warm at night. Too dazed to take much notice of prison routine, I do remember a gentle voice beside me every time I needed anything, and a helping hand guiding me to the right places at the right time. Her name was Pat, and she looked after me as a mother would look after a child. Gradually I became aware of the person herself. I couldn't have done without her love and kindness. For a long while I was afraid to touch her, or even to sit down on a communal chair, in case she or another person caught the evil that was exuding from me.

Every now and then in my mind, I would receive the blast of the shot gun, instead of Christopher. Anyone who saw me involuntarily jumping back, as if in response to a blow, must have wondered whether I had lost my sanity.

I recalled the Ten Commandments, something I had not done since Scripture lessons at school – and felt that I had damned myself to hell for ever. I could not forgive myself for having committed such a terrible crime. There was no hope, no point in living with such an inner emptiness and anguish, for there was nothing to fill the one or ease the other. Sometimes it felt as though I had been broken into a thousand pieces, each one then being flung into space: no chance of my ever being put together again. Food stuck in my throat, so I didn't bother to eat. I discovered a gym for the use of inmates, and there I punished my body.

Having seen prison life portrayed on television, I shouldn't have been surprised to discover that I was now a number. But I was. Every week I stood to attention in front of the governor trying to remember it, but I was simply unable to retain figures. The more I tried, the more elusive the numbers seemed to become. It was a humiliating and degrading experience learning that I was not Jenny Davis any more. I was J75426. I thought of the imprisoned shoemaker, in *A Tale of Two Cities*, by Charles Dickens, who eventually only remembered himself as a number – and wondered if I would do the same. I am puzzled as to why I was put through this weekly ritual over my number. It must surely have been obvious that the procedure caused me great distress, and that I was not forgetting on purpose.

My own solicitor and I decided that, as he was a family friend, it would be an unfair burden for both of us if he were to represent me. I know now that this was the right decision, as he and his wife have been able to give me the most immense support in so many other equally important ways. He continued to visit me in prison, and on one occasion asked me a question which was to have far-reaching consequences. 'Would you like to see the vicar?' he said. I was rather taken aback. Not being a church-goer, I had never met our local vicar. Out of politeness I answered, not really caring one way or another, 'He can come if he likes.'

I was in the gym when the message was brought through: 'You have a visitor.' I was slightly puzzled as this was out of visiting hours, and even more puzzled when, on being taken into a small room in the hospital wing, I saw my visitor – a stranger to me – sitting on the other side of a desk. At first I wondered if he was one of the endless stream of psychiatrists, probation officers or other similar officials involved with prisoners. But then he told me he was the vicar from our parish. Why had he bothered to come, I wondered; I was not one of his flock.

We were left alone together. I cannot remember what we spoke about, but I do remember that I couldn't stop sobbing and found it impossible to put my feelings into words. I was offered a handkerchief but refused it, preferring the soggy tissue I clutched in my hand. He gently pressed a small edition of the New Testament into my hands and suggested that I might try going to a service in the prison chapel. I replied that I felt so evil, I feared the walls of the chapel might fall down. He assured me that they wouldn't, so with some trepidation I decided to risk it and attend.

I was greatly relieved to find that the chapel continued to stand firm, despite my entry into it. Feeling a little more confident, I took my place in the front row where all hospital inmates were put, flanked by nurses and segregated from the rest of the prison girls.

The service, which was always on a Saturday, began. I stood there, numbly, until one of the girls called out for hymn 433:

When I needed a neighbour were you there,
were you there?
When I needed a neighbour were you there?
And the creed and the colour and the name
won't matter:
Were you there?                    *Sydney Carter*

As we sang, tears rolled down my face. Unable to
control my emotions, I cried out to God, this God
whom I had ignored in every respect, 'Why were you
not there? Why have you betrayed me?' My sense of
having been deserted, of being utterly alone, was so
intense that I could only sob. A lump still comes into
my throat whenever I hear that hymn, and it takes
me straight back to that prison chapel.

At the end of the service we were quickly escorted
out, and I was not allowed to stop and thank the
chaplain. When I started to attend regularly, I realised that being hurried in and out was normal. It
seemed to suggest that the whole thing was a terrible
nuisance, and that the sooner we were returned to
our cells, the sooner those in charge could get back
to the real duties of the day. Many of the girls
came to the service simply in order to get out of
their cells on a Saturday morning, and thus relieve
the boredom.

Sunday was not a day for worship, something that
I was to miss terribly on my return to Pucklechurch
after being sentenced. Instead, Sunday was a day
for scrubbing out the entire wing.

I cannot remember how often our vicar, David,
came to see me, but I do remember that one day he
laid hands on my head in the corridor as we were
saying goodbye, and gave me God's blessing. I stood

there, rather surprised, finding it very difficult to believe that God wanted me blessed in his name. At the same time there were feelings of gratitude and quiet acceptance in my heart. I began to look forward to his visits. I have forgotten what we spoke about, but the feeling of calm and security that emanated from him remains. He talked as though he really cared for me as a person in my own right. I needed that more than anything.

I was frequently called out to see the prison psychiatrist who would make me go over and over the events of the last few days of Christopher's life, trying to piece together for the prosecution what had actually happened. He always stopped short immediately after the shooting, leaving me at my most vulnerable. Although he was very courteous and kind, he didn't seem to understand that I desperately needed help with the mental anguish of my inner emptiness. No attempt was made to guide me through the pain I was experiencing. This reinforced my feeling of being, as it were, non-existent or mindless. It seemed as though I did not matter: the crime was the important factor, for all the questions I was asked related to why it had been committed.

Frantic for help, I did not know which way to turn. If I had been in a psychiatric hospital and not in a prison, I'm sure I would have received it. I felt that, at least on one occasion, I came close to insanity; certainly, it was a battle trying to stay mentally stable. Yet no one came to my rescue. One day a passing nurse, who presumably glimpsed something in the expression on my face, came in and sat on my bed, asking, 'You are not contemplating suicide, are you?' She stayed and talked to me for quite a while. She had every reason to feel uneasy about me. Without David's compassion and care, his concern to help and heal me as I was, I would certainly have tried to take my own life, not in order to opt out of the situation that I found myself in, but because life had become meaningless without Christopher. Suicide as a cry for help and as a genuine attempt to end life are very different. I had no need of a cry for help for I had no need of life. Death appeared so sweet; so attractive: it could reunite me with Christopher and take away that pain and anguish for ever. I longed for death, and felt cheated by being kept alive.

My new solicitor proved also to be an amazing man. Why he didn't walk out on me, I shall never know. A more ungrateful, stubborn client he could not have had. I certainly did not give him any encouragement. With patience and compassion he stayed by me.

An early event, minor though it may seem to others, stands out in my mind. One day, soon after we had met, when we were in one of the small interviewing rooms at Pucklechurch, I heard someone laugh. Startled at the now unfamiliar sound, I looked around to see where it had come from. Then, suddenly, it dawned on me that it was *I* who had laughed. Laughter, which had been so much part of my life with Christopher before things had started to go wrong, had deserted me in recent months. I looked with awe and respect at the man who had brought about this miracle. He had done more than make me laugh; he had won my trust.

Between them, these two men, a priest and a solicitor, gave me back faith and confidence in myself, and the will to survive: my very life and freedom. Both professionals in their own fields, they used their expertise, the one through prayer and spirituality, the other through his legal training and skills, on my behalf.

As I began to regain my sanity, I became more and more aware of my surroundings. Being in the hospital wing of a prison, meant that I was with psychiatrically disturbed prisoners. We were supervised by nurses rather than prison wardens and, provided the wing did not become too crowded, kept in separate cells. None of us from the hospital was allowed to attend educational classes. When I eventually met the person in charge of education and asked her if I could enrol in a class, I was reminded forcefully of the reason for my being in the hospital wing. I was hurt by what she said and by her manner – and felt that I should not have received the same reply if a nurse had been in earshot of our conversation. It was only later, on my return to Pucklechurch, that I learnt that those on the psychiatric wing were not considered suitable candidates for education. How Pat, my new friend, a girl of great intelligence, integrity and compassion, survived under these conditions for a year on remand, without breaking under the strain, I shall never know.

What was it that gave me new hope and a will to live? Some might assume that my children would

have been reason enough. But emotions play havoc
with a mind that has been broken and, however un-
reasonable it may seem, despite the children whom
I loved, at first I only wanted to join Christopher.
I had never known such mental anguish and never
wish to experience it again, but I found, to my total
astonishment, that people still loved me, cared about
and wanted to help me.

Letters started pouring in from people from all
walks of life. People wanted to share my grief,
show love, offer practical help and support, tell
me to hang on in there and generally encourage
me. People prayed for me.

I often looked at the little edition of the New
Testament that David had given me, wondering
whether it could hold the answer; whether it could
possibly disclose the secret of life in the midst of
death. Something inside me said, 'Read it,' but
I couldn't. My instinct said, 'Here is the key,'
but I couldn't use it. I don't know what held me
back; in any case, I found it extremely difficult to
read anything. The well-thumbed Mills and Boon
romances on offer sickened me.

Then a letter arrived enclosing a booklet, *A Time
To Pray*. The letter suggested that I should turn
to certain pages for comfort. I did, but was too
distraught for them to mean anything. It was while
I was flicking through the rest of the book, however,
that suddenly something leapt out at me. This was
a meditation on death. As I slowly read it, the
happy times Christopher and I had shared together
came flooding back, drowning the sorrow of my
present grief.

Death is nothing at all. I have only slipped away
into the next room.
I am I and you are you; whatever we were to
each other, that we are still.
Call me by my old familiar name, speak to me
in the easy way which you always used.
Put no difference into your tone; wear no
forced air of solemnity or sorrow.
Laugh as we always laughed at the little jokes
we enjoyed together.
Play, smile, think of me, pray for me.
Let my name be forever the same as it always
was.
Let it be spoken without effort, without the
ghost of a shadow on it.
Life means all that it ever meant.
It is the same as it always was; there is abso-
lutely unbroken continuity.
I am but waiting for you, for an interval, some-
where very near just around the corner.
All is well.                    *Canon Scott Holland*

I read the words over and over again, clutching at
this one crumb of comfort. They made Christopher
feel closer than he had been for a long time, not in
some morbid sense, but in a most marvellous way.
Each time I read the piece, my eyes were drawn to
the three words, 'Pray for me.' At first they were
directed at Christopher. Then, one evening, I found
I was saying, 'Father, pray for me.' Someone had
sneaked in through the back door!
The booklet was compiled by the Mothers' Union,
and it was my first taste of the wonderful strength
of that organisation within the Church of England,

about which I had never heard before. How I bless the person who sent me that book! It opened a vital door.

Soon after this, another friend sent me *A Private House of Prayer*, by Leslie Weatherhead (Hodder & Stoughton, 1958) and *Love Is My Meaning* by Elizabeth Basset (DLT, 1976). Now I was able to read them and, in doing so, discovered the miracle that God is love. I had never thought of God before in this light.

I have kept many of the letters and all the books I received during this time. The letters kept coming – from family, from friends, from people I had hardly known previously – encouraging me, giving me pictures of the outside world. In letter after letter, knowing my love of nature, friends painted verbal pictures of it for me. I heard when the snow-drops appeared, when the primroses and bluebells carpeted the woods, when the new leaves and buds burst out on the trees, when my aunt's favourite camellias opened up: one was even brought up to me from Devon. I was like a person suddenly unable to see. Those who wrote to me were my eyes.

Each letter was like opening a precious gift – a gift from the heart – and I would read it in silent wonder. I will mention two which illustrate the quality of love I was receiving.

I had always got on well with our milkman and chatted happily with him whenever I had seen him. In winter when the lanes were impassable with drifting snow (it would sometimes take three days to clear them with the snow-plough), he would walk over the fields carrying our milk – no easy task, given the distance. The contents of his letter to me in prison left me stunned. It started with an apology for writing, then went on to offer to look after my dog (a grandson of my Max buried in the garden), care for the garden or anything else I might need, and ended by saying what a privilege it would be to be allowed to help. What had I done to deserve such support?

Another such letter came from Paul, a young climbing pal of Christopher's. He wrote saying how much he would miss Christopher, but thanked me for all that I had given him. I had opened my home to him, as indeed I had to all who stayed, but the laughter and welcome in our house had been particularly precious to him, although I had not consciously given him anything special. He continued to write, sharing with me anecdotes of his exploits and incidents to make me laugh. No blame or bitterness were in his letters, although he had done so much with Christopher; only encouragement for me to stand firm and see it through.

I cried over some letters, laughed over others. The strength they gave me is without measure. I felt: If all these people care, how can I let them down? I started to write back – to well over a hundred people – sharing my darkness and grief but trying to comfort them too, by recounting little amusing anecdotes from prison life to make them smile or shield them from the starkness of that life. My solicitor was as astonished as myself when I told him of this wonderful support I was being given.

I sat alone in my cell reading these letters over and over again, amazed at the love their writers were giving not just to me, but also to the rest of the family. This great caring community looked after my children, corresponded with my brothers and sister, visited my parents, and shared with each other. I had seen on television and in the paper how tragedies and disaster brought other people together. Now I watched, with awe, this miracle happening to me in my situation.

My cell was always filled with flowers. I felt quite guilty about this for one is not allowed to share with others in prison, but they were a wonderful reminder of the love, strength and beauty on the other side of the prison gates, as well as giving me something lovely, alive and growing inside the same room as myself. I gazed at the flowers, some cut, some growing in pots, breathed in their scent, and marvelled. They seemed so clean and pure, so fresh and fragile. They were able to contribute by simply being what they were. Could people, I wondered, give so completely just by *being*, rather than doing?

I don't know when the urge to take communion stole over me. I just know it was my way of saying thank you to God for his acceptance of me; for underpinning me with so much love; for showing me how, broken in spirit, I could lean on his spiritual strength. The more I wondered at this source of strength, the greater and deeper it seemed, until it became too vast a well for me to plumb. I did not ask for forgiveness, for I did not believe I deserved it: I simply wanted to give as I had been given to.

So, one day, I asked if we could receive communion at our Saturday services. No, came the reply: time would not allow for this. It was as though I had asked for the moon. However, I was allowed a visit from the prison chaplain. He came to my cell, and we spoke through the grill on my door, which remained unopened. He said, 'I've never had a request for a visit before.' I was shocked, and felt I must have misunderstood him. Surely others must have needed a chaplain at one time or another in the past. I made my request known, and he promised to try and hold a communion service on another day. Presumably I had asked for something unusual, something requiring administrative work, because it was three weeks before anything happened. By then I was beginning to feel as though I was being a thorough nuisance.

Finally, the staff collected the names of all those wishing to receive communion. Some thought the idea a joke, a good excuse to get a taste of alcohol. Eventually half a dozen of us were taken over to the chapel to participate. I was very disappointed with the service. I felt that many of the important parts of it were cut out, and I wondered whether the chaplain had been told to keep the proceedings as short as possible. It seemed to me that the whole thing had been rushed, and I had been given no time to worship God in a eucharistic setting. I was nearly in tears when I returned to my cell. In my three months in Pucklechurch, I was only able to receive communion twice.

Being on remand, one is allowed a short visit daily. This is quite unsettling emotionally; thirty minutes every other day would probably be kinder, though administratively harder. I was moved by the numbers of people who were prepared to go through the prison gates, simply to come and show their love and concern for me. My parents were wonderful:

they didn't turn their backs on me in shame and humiliation, as they could so easily have done. My mother rose to the occasion by making a visiting rota. This meant that everyone had to contact her and my father, so they had something really positive to do; also they didn't have to keep their feelings hidden or bottled up, but were able to talk about and share their grief, distress and bewilderment with all who rang – a valuable way to help in the healing of any inner wound.

As I look back at what I was given – I who had done something so shocking and terrible – words are quite inadequate to express my feelings. There was a greatness and an outpouring of generosity and love which I could feel and from which I gathered strength. A whole range of emotions – including incredulity, thankfulness, unworthiness – welled up inside me, but I was unable to express them coherently.

This surrounding love and support sustained and carried me through the horrors of the next few months. Many times I felt that the strain would break me as I found myself teetering on the knife-edge of insanity. But as I drew on that surrounding love and support, an inner strength always came to my aid and a will-power inside me told me to hang on, as I fought a battle such as I'd never fought before.

Once I had recovered from the initial shock of what had happened, I tried to take in both my present situation and the devastation I had caused – though I found this almost impossible to handle. I now found myself living in a group which, though I had never come across it, I had always despised and assumed that its members were getting their just deserts. Never in my wildest dreams had I imagined that I would be part of such a group. I kept hoping, at first, that I was having a bad dream from which I would wake up, but I had to come to terms with the reality of the situation.

Being on the hospital wing at least meant that, although a nurse could observe me at any time, I could have the privacy of my own cell. I needed this. But if I had had hopes of finding peace and quiet, it was soon shattered. Sometimes a prisoner would bang her head against a cell door for hours on end, until the sound became unbearable and she would be taken away to the padded cell to cool off. Sometimes I would listen to uncontrollable sobbing or hysterical screaming; to tunes that were sung over and over again until they became tuneless, or to swearing such as I had never heard before. It was heart-rending. I saw alcoholics and drug addicts going through the most appalling withdrawal symptoms, until I thought they wouldn't be able to take any more. Why were these people here? What had happened in their lives to bring them to this? With sights, sounds and questions like these – there could be no peace.

If we were lucky, and if there were enough nurses to supervise us, we were allowed to attend meals at the upper end of the dining-room instead of eating locked up in our cells. Occasionally one of the girls went berserk. The emergency button was pressed and six wardens bore down on the unfortunate girl and dragged her out to the padded cell, often giving her an injection to keep her quiet. Everyone else watched uneasily, but passively.

After these episodes, those in the hospital wing would not be allowed back into the dining-room for a few days.

The only chance of speaking with other prisoners not in the hospital wing was in the gymnasium, but only if a nurse was available to accompany us could anyone from our wing go there.

During the week, in the mornings, those of us in the hospital had supervised therapy. We were allowed to draw, colour, sew or knit. But heaven help you if a needle was found to be missing at the end of the session! Everyone was searched and nobody allowed to leave the room until it was found. I remember making a stuffed animal for Victoria, but I was so inept at making toys that it ended up with squint eyes!

I found the lack of mental stimulation very hard, and asked if we could have some games such as Scrabble, Monopoly, chess or draughts. After much hesitation, brand new games were produced. Like a starved animal falling on its food, I pounced on these. It was good to play something constructive with another human being, and receive the odd half-hour of enjoyment. By concentrating on the game in hand, I could forget for a few precious moments where I was.

In the afternoons for a short while, if there were enough staff, we were allowed what was known as wing association, when we mixed together. I often just sat in my cell with the door open. The fact that it was open was a big enough bonus for me, since I have never been good in enclosed spaces. Nobody spoke much about themselves, and conversations were very limited.

The only other times our cells were unlocked were every morning for a brief time of exercise, and for cleaning. Certainly no home would ever be scrubbed daily from top to bottom as our cells were, until not one grain of dust or dirt was visible anywhere. I discovered places to dust that I had never thought about before. This fanatical and amazing ritual was one way of passing the time. On Sundays the wing was divided into sections with each inmate responsible for cleaning one particular area. We took it in turns to clean out the padded cell. I dreaded going inside: I imagined the distraught faces of all the girls who had been in there; this, and an eerie feeling that the door might close on me as I was cleaning, kept me on tenterhooks. As the cell was soundproof, I had visions of being shut in there until someone should happen to notice that I was missing.

Perhaps a predictable side-effect of what I had gone through, was that I became extremely sensitive to aggressive behaviour and to any sudden movement or noise. When I eventually got bail, the sound of a telephone made me jump in alarm; and, once, on seeing two dogs growling at each other, I felt quite hysterical.

Because of my sensitivity to noise, I eyed warily the emergency bells, placed in every possible strategic position in the prison. But one particular Sunday I found myself between two people who, armed with brooms, were about to go for each other. In a panic, I rang one of the emergency bells. As a result, everyone was locked in except me, and I was given the task of cleaning the rest of the top landing single-handed, and then given a ticking off. I was not popular with the two girls who had been deprived of a good 'set to', but they soon very good-naturedly forgave me.

Regardless of our various backgrounds, everybody was kind and helpful to each other. I found this camaraderie very touching, and tried to speak of it to one of the prison officers. She only laughed and said my trouble was that I only looked for the good in people, whereas she had learned to see the bad. I have never forgotten her remark, which I find to be not merely sad but tragic.

It is not only what happens in the prison itself that one has to contend with, but with what is going on outside, in relation to family, relatives and friends. For me, an awareness of their heartbreak and distress, and of my own powerlessness to do anything about them, was worse than anything else. Suddenly I longed to see Charlie and Victoria. The older two, having their own transport, were supporting me with regular visits. The school that Charlie had been attending was marvellous. After the tragedy, they had immediately taken him in as a boarder, and were looking after him in the most remarkable and sensitive way. Knowing how important it was that we should see each other, they brought him into the prison to see me. I am full of admiration at the great care with which they handled the situation. No family could have given him more support than they did.

Richard and Michael both being adult had homes of their own, but the younger two were now based with friends of Christopher. They lived on a farm, and while Victoria remained with them, attending school as a day pupil, Charlie only stayed with them during the holidays. Sadly these friends felt it would be unwise for Victoria to enter a prison, not knowing the heartbreak this decision would cause us both. They tried to get my agreement from prison that they should have custody care and control of both children until the outcome of my trial was known; and that in the meantime no member of my side of the family should seek to remove them. At one time they considered applying to the Court for an order. Letters from Victoria, who was only nine, were all dictated. She was made to write and say how happy she was with them, and never allowed to say that she was missing me and wanted to see me. Later she told me that after writing these letters she would go off somewhere alone and sob her heart out. All letters to her were opened before she received them, so she never knew if any were held back. But the bond of love that was between us could not be broken. Our relationship was cemented so strongly that it was able to weather all things, however painful.

My parents discovered what was happening and became quite distraught at the possibility of losing their grandchildren. I think this was the cruellest blow that I ever received. I am only grateful that the school at which Charlie was boarding thought differently. At least I was able to see him regularly.

My application for bail and Christopher's funeral had been planned for the same day. I cannot praise the prison enough for their help in this matter. They had a car standing by at the magistrate's court to take me to the funeral, in the event of bail not being granted, and provided time permitted this. My family made similar arrangements in the event of bail being granted. I sat in the courtroom while others decided my fate. Vital time ticked by as tension mounted inside me. Eventually bail was turned down, but it had taken so long to decide the matter that it was now too late to get to the funeral. I didn't know how much more emotional hammering I could take, as I fought to survive this latest blow.

I returned to prison drained of energy but, once there, a surprise awaited me. Instead of having to go through the ghastly routine of being stripped and searched, getting washed and into night clothes and then being locked up for the rest of the day, I was gently taken into one of the small interviewing rooms near reception. There, waiting for me, knowing what a terrible day it had been, was the prison chaplain. He had specially prepared a short funeral service. This was a recognition of the importance of my need, a final act of remembrance. There was no coffin and no Christopher, so with the pain in my heart almost at breaking-point, the two of us quietly went through the service and prayed together. I shall never forget the thoughtfulness of both the prison and the chaplain in this matter. For once protocol had been put aside. In the quietness of that time, I offered Christopher's and my own life to God. Then I was returned to my cell, a numb peace pervading my being for a time.

One of my brothers and Charlie attended the funeral. Victoria was considered too young. I was reminded of my own father's death and of the mistaken fear adults have of sharing such matters with children, and particularly of their failure to realise how much this physical act of remembrance plays in a child's acceptance of the reality of death. At the very least the children could have provided support for each other. Not until she read this chapter, years later, was Victoria able to speak fully and freely to me about this period in her life.

How did I live with my inner pain? Sometimes I longed to hurt myself physically to see whether this would bring relief from it. I was on the verge of discovering that I was not alone in my agony, but for the time being, despite the love that was being poured on me from family and friends, I had to learn to live with it single-handed, as it were. It is difficult to think back to this time before I had confidence to throw myself at the feet of Christ, to abandon my whole being to him in complete trust, relying on his strength alone to see me through the darkness. Although I was not aware of it, God was holding me up, waiting patiently for the time when I would turn to him in true penitence, so that I might live again, not free from pain, but with the ability to grow through it. At the time, recognising there was a God of love and of strength, but unable then to lean on him, I learned to live with my pain; it almost seemed impossible to imagine that I would ever be free of it again. However much I tried to run away and escape, I couldn't do it. Like my own shadow, it couldn't be shaken off: it was a part of me. So I learned to think coherently through it. Constant toothache is an analogy that comes to my mind. When one feels that kind of pain, how difficult it is to concentrate on anything else at all! Even the simplest things, related to ordinary everyday living, become an enormous effort. But such things have to be managed.

Through the agony of those two months in prison,

Pat looked after me, listening, comforting, encouraging and sharing with me her own terrible tragedy. She always appeared to be so strong but, in reality, underneath she was as vulnerable as I, and hanging on for dear life too. We became close companions and spent as much time together as we were allowed, often playing Scrabble, or simply sitting and chatting, as she knitted away. I knew that here was one friend that I didn't ever want to lose.

I found myself missing the simple things that we take for granted in life: being able to go to the lavatory instead of sitting on a pot; knitting or sewing when I felt like it – doing these things out of supervised time needed special permission, which was only granted for short periods, since needles were dangerous objects; using scissors or a nail file – teeth had to do instead; having access to paper – any books we used had every page numbered, and were frequently checked to make it impossible to pass notes or keep what we wrote private. Diaries were forbidden.

Thank goodness, on remand we were able to write as many letters as we wished. This became my lifeline and it never worried me that all outgoing and incoming mail was read, for I had nothing to hide. I did not realise, in my innocence, that all addresses were checked and added to a compiled list for every prisoner. My list caused much aggravation owing to its length and, as each letter was not only read but checked against the list, started to disintegrate with usage! I heard rumours that, once convicted, the ration was two letters a week. The idea was so appalling that I preferred not to think about it.

I was on remand in custody from 12th January to 4th March, nearly two months, and every day it felt as though piece by piece parts of me were slipping away out of control. Each week I had to make the journey to the magistrates' court. The prosecution were determined that I should not get bail, regardless of my circumstances. It was all so unreal, as I sat there wondering if it was really me they were talking about. Often my friends would come and support me in court, and my parents always did.

One incident in the courtroom I shall never forget. It stemmed purely from compassion and love. The prosecution was arguing its case against bail once again, painting me so evil and callous that I couldn't believe what I was hearing, when I was distracted by movement on the other side of the courtroom. A great friend of mine was being restrained from trying to leap up to protest and protect me. Sitting silently, as instructed, I wished I could hug her for wanting to affirm the true 'me'.

Despite the court appearances and the hassle, I welcomed the weekly break from prison routine. On every occasion, I departed from prison in pristine condition, having had a bath and washed my hair. Before leaving, carrying all my possessions in plastic bags as though a refugee, I was checked out completely and then solemnly handed over to the police whose property I became and who again checked me – item by item. I imagine this was very aggravating, time-consuming work for the police, especially when they were busy or short staffed, but they were always polite and courteous to me. On my return the procedure would be reversed: possessions checked, bath, hairwash and inspection.

On balance, the bonuses outweighed the inconvenience. As well as being clean and well-scrubbed, at the magistrates' court I was able to see both my parents privately in an ordinary room, while waiting for the court appearance. Instead of sitting with my hands on a table as at prison visiting times, I could get up, walk about without restriction, and hug my parents when I wanted to. There was no table between us, and we could hand each other letters in complete privacy. I was able to give them things I had made for the children, such as my stuffed lamb with squint eyes! All these things were touches of normality which the outside world takes for granted. It was as though I were, for that length of time, on an island, flying a tattered white flag marked 'TRUCE HERE'. Those precious few minutes together were worth everything.

Just being driven between the prison and the magistrates' court revived me. I saw our house in the distance, across some fields. I viewed it with curiosity, as though it already belonged to someone else.

I was well looked after by the policewomen, never locked in a cell and always given something good and hot to eat. Neither was there any hurry to return me to the prison, and this made me feel a little more human.

The transport arrangements, however, seemed strange to me. I was driven from the prison to court in a taxi, but returned to prison in a large police van. The latter is fairly conspicuous and I always felt exposed and vulnerable while travelling in it. But, to my relief, I never caught sight of any friends as we drove slowly through the town. Once, in the van,

I was offered some spray scent by a policewoman. This spontaneous gesture really touched me. There were many such kindnesses, usually offered when I least expected them. I think the loveliest of these was the suggestion that I should pretend to be handcuffed – rather than actually being so – on arrival and departure from the magistrates' court.

I soon learned that the prison and the police force were two different administrations. It almost appeared as though the police tried to outdo the prison administration and vice versa, along the lines of: 'Treat with care and ensure departure in better condition than on arrival!' There was a kind of tension between the two which quite amazed me. I had always lumped the police and prisons together, without giving much thought as to how it all worked. But then I had never been involved before!

As the chance of seeing Victoria became bleaker by the day, it became vital that I should get bail before the children could be made wards of court and I lose custody of them. I found the whole situation totally incongruous and realised what it meant to be a non-person – only a number with no rights.

A second and final application for bail was made. Only my nearest friends were informed about this and those who were putting forward financial security. Here again, the generosity of those who cared so much quite overwhelmed me; I think my solicitor was equally moved that so many people were willing to help. The amount offered was far beyond what was needed. I knew that one couple, very dear friends of mine, whose security was accepted, couldn't afford what they were offering. When I questioned them about this afterwards, they simply said, 'Jenny, we would have sold everything for you.' I asked myself, 'Would I be willing to go that far for someone else?'

There were three stipulations and conditions which I had to comply with in order to get bail: reside with either couple of the friends who had come to court to say they would let me live with them; report to the police station twice a week; return to Pucklechurch for further examination. These, I felt, shrank into insignificance compared with what I was fighting for.

What was most unusual was the presence of the prison psychiatrist in court. He had come to give evidence in support of my application for bail. I am told that without his evidence I would have had little chance of being granted bail. It was feared that I was so distraught that I might take my own life and possibly the lives of the children rather than leave them orphaned. All I am sure of is that had I not been granted bail, I would have tipped over into insanity.

There were tough times ahead but relief flooded through me as I looked forward to seeing my daughter at last, knowing that bail gave me the right to be responsible for my children again. I now had complete control over their welfare and, with my solicitor, was able to make practical provision for their future.

The agonies of the previous two months had taken their toll on my health. Under such immense strain, I had lost two and a half stone in weight, but I was free – after a fashion and for a while.

Pain and suffering, which are so destructive in

themselves at first glance, can be transformed by love and even, in time, made into something beautiful. This I was beginning to experience. Just as cuttings thrust into the soil need the gardener's tender care, so people uprooted by some tragedy need love's healing and transforming touch in their pain and insecurity. Then, given time, they can put down new roots and show new growth.

Sadly, some people find no loving hand outstretched to them in their need. So their bewildered 'Why me?' tips over into resentment and bitterness. For those two months on remand in prison, that essential loving hand was held out to me. In agony, I dimly recognised what I was being offered, and took it.

# 5

## The Cost of Bail

'And know you not,' says Love, 'who bore the blame?'

*George Herbert*

To walk out free, yet not free; to know that there would be a matter of months in which to prepare the children for what would eventually happen when this wasn't even known to me; to put one's house in order and prepare for something unknown – all this felt to me like living in a land of shadows. An unreal quality persisted throughout my four months on bail. I know that I could not have survived as I did without the love of my parents, family and friends; a love such as I had never encountered before; it involved patience, giving, asking nothing in return. At the same time, it was torture to watch, helplessly, the pain that the children and the rest of my family were having to endure through me.

Yet already I had learned so much, and I was aware that I was not alone in any of it. There was a new dimension to my life, and from within a strength flowed. I was discovering, falteringly, the importance of opening up, of relying on and putting my trust in God, as I groped my way towards the truth.

I stayed the first week with one of the couples acceptable to the court, and as they drove me to their home, I could hardly believe, after the strain of the last two months, that I was about to see Victoria for the first time since the ghastly tragedy had happened. Knotted up inside with tension, I was terrified that she would not be there.

I need not have worried, for everything went smoothly and, with utter relief flooding me, I could only thank God that we were at last together again. The handling of the situation by the school and the love and care shown by the family with whom I was staying, were wonderful. Victoria and I had been given a bedroom to share, a lovely room, fresh, cheerful and welcoming. A little pot of primroses and other spring flowers had been placed on the table. There were large soft towels, and linen sheets and pillow-cases on the beds. A special supper had been beautifully cooked, and I felt quite guilty that my diminished appetite prevented me from showing my appreciation of it. Best of all, I couldn't keep my eyes off my daughter, as though I needed constant proof that she was really there. It was so good just to be together again, and by the expression of relief on her face, I knew she felt the same.

There was a sense of wonder, too, as I was able to walk into the garden through an unlocked door and gaze at all the beauty still there. I drank everything in, knowing that this was to be the stillness and peace before the coming storm.

As I look into my garden now, it is spring again and seven years have passed. I can see one of my favourite blue primulas in bloom. It came from that very garden, given to me as a gift by my friends. I have split the plant many times over the years, in order to share it with others.

It was not long before I was able to see Charlie too, and for a few precious days I put aside the future. As the school had been so supportive and had brought him to see me in prison, I was far more relaxed about meeting him again. By their love and actions, the children showed their very real need of me, and simply being together made our happiness seem, for a time, complete.

The quiet and solitude of the surrounding country-side and the walks through the fields; the normal routines of everyday life; caring for the animals, the sheep, chicken, ducks, rabbits and dog: these were essential first steps on my road to recovery as well as contributory in building me up to face the way ahead. My health had been badly impaired, and my spirit broken. Every ounce of strength I possessed would be needed over the coming months.

Strange as it may seem, it was in my very weakness that I found strength: it was only in the knowledge of my own vulnerability that I was able to turn to God. If I had not been broken, if I had not recognised my pride and stubbornness as the barrier, I would have remained completely blind to what was being offered to me.

It's a frightening thought that the offer of help has always been there for everyone but, preoccupied with our secular lives, most of us fail to recognise it.

One of the first things I did on my release was to go and see David, who had walked into my life in prison. He saw at a glance that I was not well, and I was given quite a homily about my reluctance to see my doctor about feeling depressed. I had the idea that anything other than physical illness was a sign of weakness, but was made to realise that the mind and soul, or spirit, are just as important, and need guidance and healing in exactly the same way as does our physical being. As David knew and I needed to grasp, each of us is a unity of body, mind and spirit, and just treating one bit and ignoring the rest is counter-productive, since one aspect affects another.

I made an appointment to see my doctor, one that I should have made three months earlier. Without his care and medical treatment, combined with the spiritual guidance from David – the two aspects now went hand in hand – I could not have coped with all the other issues.

The first Sunday after my release on bail, I walked into our parish church. I felt strange: as though free to move about without being escorted by prison wardens or nurses, yet on loan to society, which, ultimately, had my freedom in its hands.

I had only been to this church once before, for a Remembrance Service a few years earlier. At Christmas and Easter it had been our custom to attend the larger one in the near-by town. I felt terribly afraid, for although I didn't know the people, some of them would most certainly recognise me, and might already have judged me. I wondered what their reactions would be. Would they turn away or simply ignore me? Strangely enough, it never occurred to me that there would be hostility.

Maybe I felt a church community was exempt from such feelings!

Shaking and trembling, I entered. The urge to worship in the community was stronger than my fear, and my feet carried me forward, even though my heart wanted me to run away. I need not have worried. There was no condemnation. I was welcomed in and, with a flood of relief, knew that I had come home.

I was coping with so many aspects of my life all at once that it is very difficult to decide how to put them into any sort of meaningful order. Reluctantly, I felt that I had to leave my peaceful existence and move back nearer to the hub of things – to my parents, the schools, my house, the police station and all the other situations that had to be faced. It was very tempting simply to bury my head in the sand and try to pass the next few months by withdrawing completely from my responsibilities, for I knew the future was going to be painful. But I also knew that I could never live with myself if I were to be so cowardly.

That first week was an important factor towards my recovery. I then moved to the home of my other friends who had offered me accommodation. They had a spacious house, where I hoped we wouldn't be continually tripping over each other. It was quite an undertaking on this family's part to offer their home to us for several months, and I was very aware of the fact that there would be times when they would need the space and time to be on their own.

I felt that reporting to the police station twice a week took up a lot of precious time which could have been used more constructively. It was not easy to stand in a queue alongside people looking for lost property, filing complaints, reporting thefts, or doing any of a hundred and one things; even harder was having to state, in a voice clear enough for everyone to hear, my reason for clocking in. At first, because of my own distress and my fear of further distressing the children, I went through the ordeal on my own. But by the end of my four months I was taking in not only my own children but also any others for whom I happened to be responsible at the time, rather than leaving them in the car for ages. I still found this experience distressing, but in time learned to accept it, as did the children. I often wonder what the police thought as they saw me trailing into the station with three, sometimes four, nine-year-olds!

One of the hardest and most painful things to face, was having to let go of the children, so that if I went to prison, they would be able to stand on their own without me. Knowing my time of freedom was probably limited, I wanted to spend every precious minute of the day with them. Every second counted, then passed and was gone for ever. Every day I felt that a part of me was dying.

In the circumstances, planning for the future seemed like sorting out what would happen after my death. True, I shouldn't be dead, but as good as, in that I should be watching events from behind an impenetrable wall, feeling useless and out of action. So I had to give the children as much normality and freedom as possible, regardless of personal cost, while preparing them at the same time for life without me.

The year before, Christopher and I had arranged for Charlie to go on a ten-day sailing course in Devon and this fell during my time on bail. I saw so little of him that to be parted for ten days seemed unbearable. I felt I needed to be with him. But, although it was a tough decision to make, I decided to let my son go on the course. In the event, he had the time of his life and it was a very proud young man who on his return showed me the certificate of competence he had gained.

None of this vital preparation for the future could have been made if I had not been granted bail, and I thank God that I was able to be with my children over that period. But at times the thought of future separation was almost too much. How could I say goodbye to the children to whom I had given birth, whom I had loved and brought up? How could I give them more pain after what they had already borne and expect them not only to understand but also to accept and grow through it – when I knew that I was the cause of it all? I kept on thinking of some verses in the Gospel of Luke about fathers knowing how to give good gifts to their children – not offering them a scorpion when they ask for an egg. Surely all parents know how to give their children good gifts. Yet my children were turning to me for support in the loss of their father, and what was I giving them in return?

I hid my pain from them to the best of my ability: they had to learn to be strong and independent, so I had to show strength too. As the days ticked by the thought of what lay ahead became more and more difficult; indeed, this parting from the children was the hardest thing I have ever been asked to do and it was only made possible by love.

There were many shocks that I had to absorb, and
many hard lessons I had to learn during those
months on bail. I discovered that my car had been
sold and nobody had bothered to take out my belongings first. My bank book, personal items, rug
and many other things that I had carefully bought
for the car itself – jump leads, tyre pressure gauge
and pump, spare petrol can, breakdown kit – had all
gone. There had been little security in the house too
and, when I went to look for the wedding present I
had given Christopher, I couldn't find it.

I was told our house would have to be sold
to cover debts incurred by Christopher, and the
remainder of the money put into a trust fund for
the children. This was all very well, but what were
we to live on? I discovered that a separate solicitor
had been appointed for the children, to look after
their interests alone. He wanted to sell the furniture
to put more money into the children's trust fund. I
felt it was a crazy situation, for how could we begin
to furnish another house if all our furniture was sold
and I was left with no money to replace it? Luckily,
my solicitor understood the position and brought
things to a halt. Nevertheless our beloved house
had to go, and the task of packing up and clearing
it out lay on my shoulders.

Part of me was in the very earth and would remain
there for ever; nevertheless, I had to leave the place
and I wanted to pass it on in good condition. With
sweat and toil I had created the garden and I wanted
it to be as beautiful as possible, to pass on to the
next occupiers the pleasure and happiness we had
received from this little corner of paradise.

Although it broke my heart to leave, I did so with love, not bitterness. This was only made possible through David, who led me through the pain. He was always there with the practical suggestions, even down to how to organise a tip for the rubbish. I leaned on his strength and wisdom not only for spiritual matters, but also for simple everyday concerns. I began to understand that there is no great divide between the 'spiritual' and the 'ordinary', for the whole of creation belongs to God.

Friends came to help me with the great task of moving, and there were hopeless giggles as cupboards were emptied and my 'squirrel' instincts – my response to Army life – were revealed, much to my embarrassment! I sold furniture that I knew we should not need again, and put it in a fund for the future – whatever that might hold. The rest we stored, for the same reason.

The weather was glorious, and the children ran in and out of the house as though nothing had happened. They were happy to be back on familiar territory and my feelings were not unlike theirs. Our attitude was something many people found difficult to understand. I just accepted it, though it did surprise me that I felt no dread about going upstairs into the room where Christopher had died. A friend of mine, who is very aware of atmospheres, said that she, too, had happy vibrations from the house. Animals are also sensitive to atmosphere so I found it reassuring that our dog was at home in every room. Our love had evidently been stronger than those last few nightmarish months of tension and suffering.

Giving away our dog, Benjamin, was very difficult. He was yet another part of our life together. We had bred him, watched him grow up from a puppy, loved him: he was part of our family. I was consoled by the knowledge that he was going to the best home he could possibly have. He is now, at the time of writing, twelve years old and occasionally I have an opportunity to see him. I don't know whether he still recognises me, but he always gives me a tremendous welcome when I visit, and it is good to see him so happy and part of a loving family.

An unexpected bonus as far as I was concerned, was that many people who were also suffering from emotional stress of various kinds, started to share their worries with me. Perhaps they felt that after the traumatic event I had just experienced, involving ongoing heartbreak and pain, I would understand more easily other emotional problems. So I found myself in the extraordinary position of trying to help others.

One thing I learnt during this time was that no one has the right to prejudge another's situation. From the outside, someone else's troubles may seem trivial, but to the person concerned they are not, and he or she needs as much care, love and understanding as the one whose tragedy seems to be the greater. Each person's pain is unique.

The love of my friends and family was very evident. I was asked out and occupied probably more than I really needed to be. In fact I was quite spoilt! Gradually I learned to eat again, and began to put on weight. I lost the drawn and haggard look as the colour came back into my cheeks. On the whole, I tried to hide the pain from these special people too, as we talked and laughed about ordinary things.

It was also important for me to take time out to be alone, to ponder, to think – occasionally leaving the children to spend a day without me. I shall always remember one particular day. Knowing my love of boats I had been asked by some friends if I would like a day's sailing in a Westerly. It was wonderful to be at the helm and feel the power of the wind in the sails. As we creamed through the water, the boat came alive under my feet and I became alive with it. All else was forgotten. I had a helmsman's certificate to race dinghies but had never sailed anything this big. So carried away was I by the thrill of it all, that I got rather too close to a ferry which was steaming straight for us and so had to do some fast manoeuvring to get out of the situation.

We headed for the Isle of Wight where we lay at anchor for an hour to eat lunch. My friends produced huge bowls of strawberries and cream which were delicious. It was such a bizarre situation that I couldn't help laughing as I wondered how the police would have reacted if they could have seen me as I was then – free to sail anywhere. Would they have regarded what I was doing as an infringement of my bail agreement?

The open space flirted with me, beckoned me, tempted me, and my heart sang with freedom as I daydreamed of sailing on for ever. But there had to be a reluctant return to reality – to the knowledge that even if I could, I would not run away from my situation.

The whole experience was like an oasis; and another wonderful thing was happening. There was a deepening relationship between myself and my parents, particularly my mother. I discovered the

compassionate aspects of her nature which I had
never seen before.

On the day of my committal hearing, my parents
were there supporting me as I sat in court. I clenched
my hands together trying desperately to keep them
still and appear calm, though inside me there was
sheer terror, and, at one level, incredulity: could
these people really be talking about me? I sat
between my parents, and my stepfather reached
over, putting one of his hands firmly over mine.
This had a great calming influence on me, and I felt
so proud of them both.

As requested by the solicitor for the prosecution,
during the bail application, the court now made
arrangements for me to return to Pucklechurch
prison for further examination and questioning by
the prison psychiatrist. I knew this had been a bail
condition, but I was not looking forward to being
questioned all over again. I drove over with a friend
for moral support. It was hot and we bought an ice
cream each from a van parked on the side of the
road, just outside the prison gates. The psychiatrist
drove up, just as I was taking my first mouthful
of ice cream. He came over to us and invited me
to accompany him. It seemed incongruous to be
walking through the gates, chatting away and eating
ice cream, as though this were a normal stroll on an
ordinary day.

There was an eerie silence as we walked through
to the hospital wing. I realised, with a pang, that
this was because everyone was locked away. I felt
quite uneasy about being on the outer side of the
locked doors. Everything seemed back to front, as
in Alice's Wonderland. I was offered a cup of tea

in a china cup! I found this disconcerting – a far cry from my previous experience of being given a plastic mug of tea to drink in the cell I had occupied. We then entered the psychiatrist's office, with which I was quite familiar, for we had talked together many times in this room during my stay in Pucklechurch.

He was very sympathetic, knowing that it was an ordeal for me to try and explain all over again what had happened on the night that I had shot Christopher, and why.

After a couple of hours, drained and extremely exhausted, I was relieved when told that I wouldn't have to spend a night in the prison, and I rejoined my friend, who had been waiting patiently for me, outside in the car. I could not have managed the drive back without her support.

But the ordeal was not over. I was on a murder charge, to which I was pleading not guilty, but guilty of manslaughter by reason of diminished responsibility. The prosecution needed to be satisfied that there were grounds for this plea. Because the prison psychiatrist had given evidence in my favour for bail, they wanted me to see another psychiatrist. So a few weeks later an appointment was made at the psychiatric hospital in Bristol.

I had never been inside such a hospital before. From the outside the place appeared quite ordinary. I walked through the beautiful grounds trying to find an entrance to the building. It took me quite some time to find a member of staff who was able to direct me to the right entrance, and with great relief I eventually reached my destination. Then, for two hours I was questioned again, this time by the head psychiatrist. I developed a blinding headache as I tried to go through it all again. Immediately he showed concern and sympathy, and made sure that a nurse gave me something to relieve the pain. After our interview I was looked after until I felt well enough to drive home. I had not thought to bring a companion this time, which was a mistake, and on the way back I was so exhausted that I stopped in a lay-by to sleep for a while.

In all I saw three psychiatrists, for the defence counsel also needed a psychiatric report.

Underneath all the trauma of the months on bail lay a yearning to fill the void in my being, to see the God who had lit my heart with a small flickering flame of love. Instinctively, I knew that this was the way I had to tread in order to be healed. As I wondered if I dared to ask or even hope for forgiveness for a crime for which I could not forgive myself, I trembled.

The first book that David offered me was *The Letters of Evelyn Underhill* (Longman). I had never read a spiritual book before, apart from the books on prayer sent to me in prison, and I absorbed this one like dry blotting paper soaking up ink.

I often wonder at David's decision to give me this book – one which many people find difficult to read – as my first taste of spiritual reading. But it was a wise decision. I went on to read books by Baron von Hugel, Dietrich Bonhoeffer, Thomas Merton and many others. I absorbed what was right for me and discarded the rest. I read extracts from Teilhard de Chardin, Anthony Bloom, Michel Quoist, the Taizé brothers, Simone Weil and others. An exciting new world had been opened up for me. I recognised even more clearly that to have a living relationship with God, I needed to start at the very beginning by asking him for forgiveness.

Strange though it may seem, I was in fact falling in love. My instinct to love God in return for his love was a driving force which I cannot explain. I approached David with great apprehension, for I found it difficult to understand how God could forgive my terrible act. After a short discussion and explanation on the sacrament of reconciliation, he gave me a leaflet explaining the Anglican approach, suggesting that I go home and pray about it. He advised me neither one way nor the other, simply waited patiently until I had made my decision. Someone who is accustomed to using the sacrament of reconciliation as a way of receiving God's forgiveness would probably be quite astounded at the agonies I went through trying to pluck up courage to return to David and ask him to hear my confession. Although I longed for forgiveness, I hesitated as I felt I had no right to ask for it.

At the same time, I couldn't stay away from the Eucharist. Every time I received the bread and wine, I knew I was not worthy to be there, but the love which I couldn't explain drew me to this sacrament, regardless. Each time I received the bread and wine, I saw Christ's broken body and expected to be condemned to death for what I had done. But the love received from him was worth more; my heart had already been broken when I had taken Christopher's life. There was nothing worse that I could do; therefore I stood there, accepting any judgment that might be given. I asked only to share this love I was experiencing with others.

I was aware, too, of Christ's teaching on anger, especially the passage in Matthew about making peace with your brother before offering your gift to God (Matthew 5). Although I had not picked up the Bible since my schooldays, verses would come into my mind, unbidden. It was partly because of the passage in Matthew that I hesitated to commit myself to the sacrament of confession. It seemed from those verses that in order to have a right relationship with God, I also had to have a right relationship with the people from whom I needed forgiveness. But it didn't seem possible to make peace with Christopher's family, whom I had hurt so much. What had happened was too fresh in their minds for the possibility of reconciliation just then. I could only hope that sometime in the future God would find a way to heal their pain.

In the end, my love for God overcame my hesitancy; and in exactly the same way as I had accepted the bread and wine at the altar, I offered myself to God in penitence, longing for absolution.

It was a shattering experience going back over my entire life, section by section, for this was something I had never done before with a critical eye. I wasn't sure that I liked all that I saw, but it was myself, the whole of myself that I wanted to offer to God. It took several hours of prayer and hard thinking. Writing it down so that I shouldn't evade certain areas, also helped.

All was quiet as I entered the church and approached the altar rails. As I knelt there beside the priest who had led me to this point, I was frightened. Voicing my thoughts to God in the privacy of my own heart was one thing, but I had to say them out loud, in front of another human being – something entirely different. Costly as this proved, it was nothing compared to what I was being offered by God. The magnitude of what this meant was overwhelming. The question was: Was my meagre faith – so new, so fragile – strong enough for me to be able to accept forgiveness? Could I really start again with a clean slate as from that day, regardless of what society or the world felt? My whole body trembled as these thoughts raced round in my mind. I knew God would forgive me, but could I forgive myself?

Love alone took me by the hand and led me to the altar. Love alone broke down my barriers. Love alone gave me the ability to accept forgiveness.

I cannot say that I came away leaping for joy, for I was too drained to think very clearly. But as the solemn words of absolution were given, I could doubt no more that God had forgiven me. A peace stole over me such as I had never experienced before. You cannot expect to plant a seed and watch it flower the next day: it takes time. But a miracle had happened. A seed had germinated in the depths of darkness, had broken out of its case and was beginning to stretch upwards to the light. It was only a matter of time before it would recognise that light and open up with joy.

An entirely new dimension had been added to my life.

While I had been on remand in prison Charlie had written to me saying he would like to be confirmed. I thought he was very young to take this step, but the school were reassuring, so on May 28th 1983,

he was confirmed in Holy Trinity church. The fact
that I was on bail meant that I could be with Charlie
for his confirmation. John Neale, the then Bishop
of Ramsbury, officiated and afterwards we all went
back to the school for tea.

A few days after Charlie's confirmation, I asked
both David and my solicitor if I could go into retreat
for a few days. Their reactions were interesting.
David was concerned that I might find difficulty
facing myself in prolonged silence. My solicitor was
concerned about the reaction of the prosecution, in
view of the fact that the court and the police would
need to agree to a change of address and therefore a
variation in the terms of my bail, not long before the
trial. I didn't really understand all this, but realised
my request might cause a problem.

However, I did not give up. I needed to be alone
with God. In the end, Ivy House, a convent in
Warminster, was contacted and I was allowed to
stay there for two glorious days waiting on God in
the silence of my heart, coming back to sleep the
night with the children. During our last evening in
the little chapel of the convent, we were led through
a time of meditation on our own spiritual journey.

Suddenly I had a vision of a long wide road,
roughly made. It was like a map in some ways, but it
also appeared to be a preview of a journey. On either
side of the road there were small clustered areas. At
first I thought these were villages, but no, they were
communities, pockets of warmth, of love, of rest. As
I walked along the road, I wanted to stop, and stay
in one of the areas, merge with the community and
immerse myself in the love I felt. But I was only
allowed to stay for a short while in any one place.

Then I would be taken by the hand and led back on to the road. At the end of the road was a bright light to which my eyes were continually attracted.

It was a terrible road, its surface rough, uneven and deeply rutted; a road of suffering and anguish, of darkness and despair, of loneliness. But only through the darkness could one walk towards the light.

I felt that there were many people called to walk that road, but we never met, for we all had to walk through our own personal darkness, with faith as our only guide. There was no calculable distance to the light: at one time it would blaze so brightly as to reach from one end of the horizon to the other; at another it would simply light up the end of the road. The rays never reached the darkness but were always just beyond it.

Although I felt alone, I was never in fact alone, for God was there. When the desolation grew too great, I would be led gently back to rest awhile in another area. Each pocket of warmth gave a different comfort, depending on the needs of the traveller. Towards the light, the places of rest grew fewer and fewer until there was only the one light ahead, and that light was pure love and truth. It was the road of love, of complete self-surrender to God's will, of being content in that alone.

The picture was vivid, but needed to be experienced by all the senses. It was similar to a young child's painting.

My faith was very new, only a matter of a few months, and what I saw was very confusing. How could anyone possibly tread such a dreadful path? I shuddered inside at the idea of even trying to

commit myself to such a way, for it meant letting
go of everything. I tried to put the idea aside. It
was for others who were braver and stronger, and
I was afraid.

Those two days in the convent were very special
for it was the beginning of a wonderful friendship
with the nuns that was to give me great strength
during my time in prison. They were a power
house of prayer which held me in love when I
was low. Eventually on my return from prison I
was to go back there into a five-day retreat; since
then, retreats have become an essential part of my
life – a time put aside each year for waiting on God;
a time I cannot do without.

The Eucharist was where I felt Christ's presence
most keenly. It was where I was able to offer
myself to him in complete abandonment. It was
where I received his love and strength to continue
living. And here was the problem. How was I going
to return to prison life and leave all this behind? At
times, it didn't bear thinking about, but I had to face
it, for I knew how difficult it had been to arrange two
communion services during my time in custody. I
agonised as to whether I should abstain from the
Eucharist in order to make the future deprivation
less painful, or whether to continue to receive the
sacraments and put what was to follow completely
into God's hands. Again, Biblical passages came
unbidden to my mind. One of these was in Luke's
gospel. In answer to a question about fasting, Jesus
replied that the guests at a wedding wouldn't fast
as long as the bridegroom was with them. 'But,' he
added, 'the day will come when the bridegroom will

be taken away from them, and then they will fast.'
(The last word is elsewhere translated 'mourn'.)

Sharing in the early morning weekday commun-
ions, which I did as often as possible, was the most
wonderful start to the day. I came away with a
spring in my step and a lightness of heart that put
life into proportion and gave a perspective to all
that I encountered, for it brought everything I did
into the presence of God, and was encompassed
within his love.

The pain of parting from the children became daily
more and more unbearable but my face continued to
radiate love. Some couldn't come to terms with this,
for was I not on a murder charge? Why wasn't my
head bowed down with guilt? Some said it would
go against me if I appeared in court looking so
happy. Yet others found it inspiring to see guilt
replaced by love.

The trouble with love is, that if it comes from the
heart, it is impossible to hide: and I was not going to
live a lie simply to make people feel comfortable. I
could not have hidden what I felt, even if I had tried.
It transcended all human love and was completely
out of my control. I was aware that I was causing
consternation, but simply accepted the situation, for
I was greatly in need of this strength to carry me over
the next few months. My probation officer spoke of
being disturbed by my countenance, and I could not
make him understand that my life had ceased to be
mine: that I was experiencing a love beyond verbal
description, even beyond my understanding; a love
so powerful that I could not and did not even need
to speak about it. It simply shone through me, and
I was utterly captivated by it. The germinated seed

had recognised the light of love and, through the pain, was bursting with joy.

To reveal emotions of love at such a time seems unseemly, distasteful, shocking. How terrible to be talking about love when Christopher had only just died. Would it not have been nicer to have remained silent, out of respect, in view of what had just happened? But we can't decide when God chooses to reveal himself to us, and the invitation that God had offered me was not a nice tea party!

All I can say with certainty, is that, having been forgiven so much, my heart was overflowing with love. In one of his books, Paul Tillich says, 'People are sick not only because they have not received love, but because they are not allowed to give love – to waste themselves.' He calls it 'holy waste'. We can read for ourselves the wonderful story, in Luke chapter 7, of how the woman who had sinned so much, washed Jesus's feet with her tears, dried them with her hair, kissed them and poured perfume over them.

How dare she show such a display of love! Etiquette forbade such goings-on. Besides, she was not a 'nice' woman to know. Onlookers were shocked, embarrassed and appalled at this unnecessary outrage to their feelings.

But they did not know the whole story. They felt it to be an extravagant waste that precious ointment, which could have been sold and the money given to the poor, should be poured over Jesus. But love says otherwise. Margaret Magdalen, in *Transformed by Love*, describes most wonderfully this complete love for Christ, as well as people's reactions to it. For my part, I have no doubt that love stemming from forgiveness is total. My heart still comes fully alive and alight as I read the two prayers at the end of the ASB Communion Service:

Father of all we give you thanks and praise, that when we were still far off you met us in your Son and brought us home. Dying and living, he declared your love, gave us grace, and opened the gate of glory. May we who share Christ's body live his risen life; we who drink his cup bring life to others; we whom the Spirit lights give light to the world. Keep us firm in the hope you have set before us, so we and all your children shall be free, and the whole earth live to praise your name; through Christ our Lord. Amen.

Almighty God, we thank you for feeding us with the body and blood of your Son Jesus Christ. Through him we offer you our souls and bodies to be a living sacrifice. Send us out in the power of your Spirit to live and work to your praise and glory. Amen.

I come out of church bursting to share the wonder and joy of God's love and forgiveness.

My emotions, however, continued to plunge me into the depths of despair as well as to take me to the heights. There were days when I couldn't stop crying for grief – grief for myself, for Christopher, for the children and my family. These were the days when God carried me.

Throughout, David simply got on with the practicalities of what had to be done. He was the

stabilising influence of my life. He organised the
continuing schooling of my children with the help
of the local educational authorities and a Christian
trust based in London, all of whom recognised that
a stable environment for the children who were, in a
sense, about to be orphaned, was vital. I shall always
be indebted to the trust for the care and concern they
showed for us as a family unit. They continued to
help even after I had come out of prison, giving
not only financial support until I could stand on my
own feet, but also advice on how to start coping
emotionally as I integrated back into the community.
They cared for us, asking nothing in return, and I
was overwhelmed by their true Christian giving.

One day David asked, 'What are you going to do
with yourself in prison? You cannot waste the time
away – you must use it constructively.' I had been
so busy clearing up our house, coping with my own
emotions and the children's, that this was one area
to which I had not given much thought. It might
have been because I still couldn't face up to the fact
of prison. The thought was too terrible for me. But
David was looking ahead to the future. He sent me
off to see an educationalist to discuss how I could
most usefully use my time to qualify for a job on
my return to society. Little did I know that the
ensuing discussion, which was both interesting and
stimulating would not lead to anything: education
in women's prisons was still very limited, as I was
to discover.

There were several other matters to face. I was
advised to put my children into care for their own
security, which I did. There was no guarantee that

they would be returned to me after my release from prison, as this would depend on how capable I was of caring for them then.

My crown court appearance was fixed for July 28th. If on that date the prosecution counsel and trial judge were to refuse to accept a plea of guilty to manslaughter by reason of diminished responsibility, I would have to return to court later in the year for a full trial on a murder charge – possibly sometime in December.

Very conscious – rather like a person under sentence of death – of how little time I had left, I began to see with a clarity never before experienced. Every tree, every flower, every sunset had a sharpened beauty as though I were seeing each for the last time. I savoured in my heart all that I would have to leave behind. Every part of creation became more exquisite. My heart moved with every cloud scudding across the sky. At times I thought I should break down, but the inner strength I had received kept me going.

The family I was staying with were very good. They lent me a car so that I could be mobile and independent. We moved some of my furniture to their lodge in case I should be set free in July. Otherwise, they would let the place, and the children could live with them. What more could I ask?

Five days before the trial, my sister flew in from Australia to support not just me but the rest of my family too. On that same day, while I could still think logically, I packed a bag ready for prison life. I knew that books were restricted, so I copied sayings that would help me, and stuck them into my Bible. That at least could not be taken away from me.

The day before the trial, we had lunch with some friends who lived near Shaftesbury. Elizabeth, a warm and loving person, gave me a little statue of the Virgin Mary she had had specially blessed which was to lie in my handbag in darkness for my entire prison sentence. Now it is back in the light of my room, a reminder of the love I received from everyone and of that figure standing at the foot of the cross in quiet acceptance of God's will.

The sands in the hour-glass ran out. I had tried to do everything possible to make life easier for the children. Charlie's birthday was on July 26th. We celebrated it on July 27th, the eve of the trial. I made him a cake with a chocolate pheasant on it and we had a barbecue in the garden. David came, bringing him a book on knots. I suggested to Charlie that, if I did not return the next day, he might like to ring Christopher's brother to arrange to go sailing with him.

In the evening I entered our bedroom to find Victoria lying on the bed, her little body racked with sobbing. There was nothing I could say. I held her in my arms, bleeding inwardly too. That night, I wrote in my diary for the last time sitting at the window overlooking the lovely garden. The next day my fate would be decided.

Dear God, thy will be done, I prayed.

# 6

# Back to Pucklechurch

There is no wood like the wood of the cross for
lighting the fire of love in the soul.
*Elizabeth of the Trinity*

July 28th 1983 will be a day I shall never forget.
It is difficult to write about it without feeling emotional. It was, without question, the most incredible
day of my life.

I woke early, having already decided to start the
day by praying quietly on my own in church. I could
then offer all that was to happen to God, by putting
it into his hands.

I slipped out of the house before anyone was
up. Victoria, sleeping in the bed beside me, did
not stir. It was a beautiful morning and I breathed
in the fresh summer air as I walked up the path
to the church. Although it was six o'clock and
nobody was about, for some reason I presumed
the building would be open. It was a great shock
to find the door locked, and for a while I was
quite stunned. My longing to be inside was very
great; instead, I walked round to the other side
of the church, sat on a gravestone and prayed.

Never before had I felt so intensely the beauty of the world about me. I longed to be given the chance to have my freedom and look after my children, and the words, 'Thy will be done', took on a new meaning as I offered myself and the children to the mercy of God.

I returned to the friends who had looked after us all for four months. Victoria was just waking up. There was very little to say. At nine o'clock David arrived to drive me to Bristol Crown Court, as I knew I would be quite incapable of making the journey in the company of my parents without breaking down. On this day of all days, I had to stay calm.

I said goodbye to the children. Victoria flung her arms around my neck crying, 'You will come back, Mummy, you will promise to come back, won't you?' Her hands had to be prised from behind my neck. Charlie just stood there with tears streaming down his face, saying nothing. I can feel those hands round my neck and see those tears today. It was a terrible moment.

We arrived at the court where my parents and friends were already gathering. The pain and distress on their faces was plain to see but they had come to give me support. I attempted to introduce those who had come alone to one another, so that they would not feel lonely. They were all being very brave and it struck me that this was rather like being present at one's own funeral! I looked inside the courtroom. It seemed fairly empty, apart from some members of the press and a few other people. I kissed my family and friends and we entered together.

I was sentenced to two years imprisonment for manslaughter, on the grounds of diminished responsibility. As I was being taken out of sight, the policewoman in charge of me turned and gave me a hug. I was in too much pain to say anything, and had to refuse a request from my parents to come down and see me. David, who had been instrumental in changing my life and showing me the pathway to God, came down to the small room below, blessed me, kissed me briefly on the cheek and left. It was not a time for words. I was put behind bars once more to await my return to Pucklechurch.

The press were given no chance to photograph me, for we waited until everyone had gone before returning upstairs. The van was brought round and the journey back to Pucklechurch began.

This time I would not be on remand, or experience the kindness of the hospital wing.

Every time you enter a prison you are treated as though you are contaminated. You are inspected for nits and made to bath and wash your hair; you are searched and all items of clothing are recorded. There are regulations as to what you are allowed. I was issued with these, and the rest of my belongings, including my handbag in which lay the little statue of the Virgin Mary, were taken away until the day of my release.

You are not allowed to mix with or speak to anyone before being checked in. So, if the staff cannot attend to you straight away, you are put somewhere out of reach. In Pucklechurch, there were two cubicles in the reception area, known by the inmates as 'the horse-boxes'. Each was about two foot six by three foot, with a piece of wood at the end for a seat.

I was stripped, given a very short towelling gown and locked in a cubicle. It was only long enough for me to take two small paces at the most. I found it very claustrophobic. There was a small, almost soundproof window out of which I could see a little, but nobody was allowed near the cubicles.

There is no doubt that the effects of the past four months, and the strain had brought me almost to breaking point again. There flashed before my eyes the faces of my parents and friends as we had said our poignant goodbyes that morning. I became very short of breath. All this and the fact that I cannot cope well in enclosed spaces, brought me to a state of near panic. I tried to remember how to calm down, and started counting to ten very slowly. I tried pacing but the distance was so short that it was useless. The more I tried, the worse it became until I was gasping for air. I tried to get help, for I felt I was suffocating, but no one responded. I have never felt so alone and so frightened.

It was then that I slowly started to say 'The Jesus Prayer', asking God for forgiveness for all the pain and suffering I had caused that very day: Lord Jesus Christ, Son of the living God, have mercy on me, a sinner.

What happened next I shall never understand, or even try to. I have agonised many times since then as to the reality of it, asking myself whether it resulted from shock or whether I was hallucinating. Now I question no more, simply accepting that what happened gave me a strength and love that carried me through prison in the most remarkable way. I had not heard of the Jesus Prayer until three months earlier, but since that time I have found it to be a wonderful way of stilling the mind, and making one more aware of the greatness and mercy of God.

As my being began silently to say the words, I became aware that I was not alone. I was standing before the cross. Time became immaterial. I do not know how long I stood there before my mind grasped what it was seeing, but in that moment I wanted to run away. I was conscious of my nakedness and I tried to wrap the towelling robe more tightly round my body. I pressed my back against the door in a pathetic attempt to escape or get further away but the cubicle seemed to shrink in size. I was so horribly close to the cross – a situation which, in the end, I realised that I had no option but to face.

I saw Christ's hands held by cruel nails, the blood streaked and congealed, and was rooted to the spot in utter horror. As surely as I stood there, I was a party to what had been done to him. I became acutely aware of my own sinfulness, as though I had personally hammered in the nails which held his body so firmly to the cross. Suddenly all my pain was as nothing compared to what I saw and felt.

Reluctantly I looked up and, to my amazement, saw that there was no look of horror directed at me, none of the expected condemnation. Instead, love and forgiveness flowed down and engulfed my whole being. There was a terrible sadness, but it was full of compassion as I was held in total warmth and security. The physical horror paled into insignificance compared to the greatness of that moment. At the same time I saw a light. That light was us. It was struggling for existence against

the darkness but I knew it would win, because I
had a glimpse, from within my heart, of eternity –
a time beyond time, a life beyond time – when love
would triumph. I felt a vastness of spirit beyond my
understanding. Then I was alone once more.

My whole being was on fire. I was still gasping for
air, but it didn't matter: I had ceased to be afraid.
My inner pain had been replaced by a purpose –
to share with others the love I had experienced.
Put behind bars, my heart had been set free. Imprisoned, I had been forgiven and released. When
they unlocked my cubicle, they did not know what
they were unlocking!

With my heart on fire, I re-entered a world of
bitterness, resentment, anger, betrayal, desertion
and hurt; a place where deprivation and degradation
were the order of the day; where four-letter words
were in common usage. I was part of that world.
We were the people who had become outcasts from
society, to be looked down upon. But had God
abandoned us? Weren't we the people that needed
his love the most?

The love I received broke down almost impenetrable barriers – barriers of upbringing, class and
convention. Suddenly I was able to see staff and
fellow-prisoners as of equal worth with myself
and with each other. There was no distinction.
The ability to relate without any form of prejudice
or resentment to those who had complete control
over my physical being surprised even me.

My strength and faith were to be tested to their
limit. All the useless waste, the degradation of
humanity and the tragedy which I was to see and
experience, could have turned me away from God

in bitterness and frustration. My encounter with his unconditional love and forgiveness in that small cubicle was God's way of preventing that from happening. It was as though my heart had been set alight to burn for ever. Even when life appeared to be at its blackest – and there were times when I was so low with pain that I didn't know which way to turn – nothing could take away what I had experienced and no one could kill that inner fire.

I was summoned the next day to the Governor's office. Expecting the usual procedure, I was surprised and amazed when she smiled, addressed me by my Christian name and offered me a chair. I had never sat in her office before. This was obviously not an official visit. She told me that someone in great distress, given a severe sentence on the same day as myself, would be coming into Pucklechurch. Would I be willing to share a cell with her and give her as much support as I could?

I found it difficult to believe that I was actually being asked instead of told to do something. To be given a choice does not happen much in prison. I agreed to her request. Then, as I was leaving, she said with another smile, 'I think it will be someone you know.'

It was Pat! Six months earlier she had looked after me with loving care as I had struggled to regain my sanity and make some kind of sense out of what had happened. How wonderful that I was able to give something to this girl who had given me so much! As she was brought into our cell, we fell into each other's arms. Neither of us were able to speak, for we were both crying. We simply held each other.

Every now and then her body shook with sobbing. It was terrible to see the strain in her face and think of what she had gone through. I thanked God for the strength and love that I had been given only the evening before.

On conviction prisoners are sent to a reception prison before the authorities designate the place to which they will go to serve their sentences – a procedure which takes weeks – hence Pat's return to Pucklechurch. My solicitor said I would probably go first to Holloway.

Two days after my return to Pucklechurch I was interviewed again by the psychiatrist. He began by saying how sorry he was that I had returned, and then asked where I would like to go, as though I were being given a choice of holiday. I reminded him that I was ignorant of the location of prisons, having never had cause to know about these things before. So we looked at a map on the wall together, calmly weighing up the pros and cons of each prison. Askham Grange, in Yorkshire, came out top. One of its advantages was that it was within two hours' drive of my brother. Another was that it was an open prison, which in theory meant more freedom for the prisoners – something that the psychiatrist felt I needed. I am grateful for his efforts on my behalf, and my solicitor was quite astonished that I should have been dealt with so compassionately.

It was to take three months to arrange my transfer to Askham Grange and in the meantime it was a waiting game with time to take stock of my surroundings.

As I have mentioned before, I find enclosed spaces extremely difficult to deal with. In the hospital wing there had been a cell per person and therefore some kind of privacy. Here, things were completely different. The cells were crammed together down either side of dark, narrow, airless and stuffy corridors. Each cell was tiny with a barred window in which was only a long opening, three inches wide: a space too small for a plastic mug to be pushed through but big enough to allow Pat and me to throw out crumbs to the birds.

That July it was very hot: a drought was eventually declared. I was still suffering from shock and felt that I needed to get my face into the fresh air in order to breathe, but this was an impossibility and so I found it very difficult not to panic. It was worse at night. For several days and nights it was a nightmare as I gasped for air in that stuffy cell. I begged the staff for help. I'm sure even a spot of vapour for colds might have helped, but none of them seemed to care.

Many other shocks were to come, but the worst for me was the lack of privacy. In a prison, physical privacy is virtually impossible. My craving for it became intense – so intense that I was forced to examine this concept that most people in the outside world take for granted, in order to come to terms with my situation.

To sit on a pot in front of another person, when brought up to feel that natural functions should be performed discreetly and in private, is indeed a lesson in humiliation. I held out as long as possible, causing myself a lot of discomfort. In such a situation, constipation was not surprising and in desperation one evening, I asked for some pills for this condition and ended up with diarrhoea. I have never felt so degraded as, when having filled up my own pot, I had to ask Pat if I could use hers. We had to sleep with the resulting stench the entire night, in relentless heat and with almost no fresh air.

To begin with I could not think beyond the lack of physical privacy, which I found intolerable. I remember begging to be locked in alone in my cell while the others were 'in association' – that is, in a room where we could mix, under supervision, once a day. This had a television, chairs and a ping-pong table. It was always incredibly noisy and full of smoke which was especially hard for a non-smoker to stomach. But everyone there was extremely kind to me and I was included in every discussion.

My request to be left in the cell while the others met in association was granted only once and probably in error: I am sure it went against security and the precautionary measures governing the safety of prisoners. But that time for me was a treasured pool of stillness, a time to pray and to be alone with God, a memory to last me through Pucklechurch.

Gradually I was able to see my body as only one aspect, albeit an important one, of my being, and to be even more aware of the need for *inner* privacy. And here a shock awaited me.

I realised that, by letting God totally into my life, inner privacy had gone by the board; that never again would I be alone. This was disturbing. In most people's lives, and certainly in mine, there are times when we either do or think things of which we are ashamed. I certainly wouldn't want anyone else to know about some of my thoughts and actions. So the knowledge that God knew these things made me begin to think more carefully about what I did and said and I tried, not always successfully, to be utterly sincere with myself and with others. There was no point in trying to have two sets of values, one on the outside and one on the inside, when God knew what went on in both areas!

I do not know whether a person brought up to accept Christ as a living part of their lives from their earliest years would receive quite such a jolt as I did, but the effect was greater honesty, and acceptance of myself, warts and all, in God's presence where pretence is useless. Strangely enough, knowing that we can never hide anything from God can also give an immense sense of freedom and joy as we are released to be our true selves. We know also that God is there to uphold and strengthen us in times of difficulty and stress, and this knowledge can bring the most wonderful comfort.

God's presence can also make us more aware of our vulnerability and of our failings despite our good intentions. However, since he is a God full of love and compassion, we have only to turn to him with penitent hearts to be freely forgiven and to experience a love and companionship that are beyond measure. He becomes the still small voice or the silent stillness, in among the noise and rush of everyday life. He can bring cohesion and stability to any situation or person; he can give light in the darkness.

My inner privacy with God, which no one can take away, helped me to find that stillness and to learn to cope better with the lack of physical privacy.

If anyone had told me beforehand that in prison conditions would be so physically humiliating in an age when human rights are a major issue, I should probably not have believed them. But such was the case.

A particular concrete room stank of drains and it was in here that difficult prisoners were put as a punishment. I would never consider keeping an animal in such dark and unhygienic surroundings, and I am disturbed to think of people still being put in that cell, for all I know.

Sadly, women's prisons are kept very much under wraps. As a result, little is known about them, which means that few, if any, improvements are made. I thought the rumours of the lack of hygiene that had filtered over to the hospital wing could not possibly have been true, but I was mistaken. It is not surprising that there is unrest.

Each night we filled a bucket with water, for our morning ablutions or for drinking. Teeth, body, hair, underclothes had to be washed in this. How did one choose which took priority? There were no basins or drains in the cells, so it wasn't possible to use the water a bit at a time, then pour it away. Ironically there were wash-basins with running water at the end of each corridor, but these were used only once a day; not for us the privilege of turning on a tap for running water – something which all of us do in our daily lives without thinking about it.

I was caught one evening washing my underclothes in the basin after doing my teeth, prior to filling up my bucket for the night. If I did that again, I would be put on report, I was told. All clothes were to be washed once a week on a rota system, under supervision. Baths were also a once-a-week privilege, and yet we were continually being given lectures on the importance of hygiene to health.

Still, every system has its loopholes. There was one job that entitled the lucky prisoners to have a daily bath – and that was working in the kitchen. Both Pat and I requested to work there and were allowed to. Although at the end of the day a bath of a few inches only was allowed, we found this a luxury, and were thus able to keep clean. Even in the bath, or in the lavatories – when we were allowed to use them – there was no guarantee of privacy, for anybody could look over the half-doors at any time. Despite this, I managed to wash essential underwear in secret, hiding it in a towel to dry, and often putting it on damp. Damp clothes were better than dirty ones!

Although Pat and I worked in the kitchens, the food was actually cooked in the men's side and brought over in a hot trolley. We then transferred it to the hot cupboards in our kitchen. It was a fairly unsatisfactory way of keeping the food warm.

One day when we were transferring the food, I noticed that it was marrow stuffed with rice, but the marrow was raw and cold. Obviously a mistake had been made but, rather than admitting this, the wardens told us that this was the way the dish should be. They continued to declare, adamantly, that the marrow was always like that, even though they gave us extra bread to fill up on while the meal was quietly removed. The action of giving us the bread, it seemed to me, was a tacit admission that the meal was inedible. It would have been so much simpler, I felt, to admit openly that a mistake had been made.

All our plates and cutlery were made of plastic, presumably for safety reasons. And at the end of each meal when we had washed and dried up, every knife, spoon and fork had to be accounted for. I suppose the routine became a habit, but sometimes we found ourselves waiting for what seemed ages for an officer to return and check the cutlery. The plates were red plastic, and the cutlery was of the white picnic type that snapped easily. There were no small spoons, so eggs were eaten with fingers, or peeled and sandwiched between slices of bread. Bread was used for everything.

Occasionally we got so bored that if the passage-way to the side of the dining-room was clear, with no warden in sight, we used the plates as frisbies, seeing if we could get them to fly the full length of the room. As the entire length between the passage and dining-room was glass (presumably strengthened), this enabled any passing staff to check our movements at a glance. At other times we ran flat out from one end to the other, leaping in the middle to see if we could touch the ceiling. I was always unsuccessful, although Pat managed it quite easily. From the outside it may all seem very childish, but we learned to find amusement in very simple ways.

I was struck quite forcefully by the thought that wherever there is suffering and deprivation, humour has an amazing way of coming to the fore. It provides a safety-valve for people living abnormal lives and suffering in different ways for different reasons.

I remember the first time I saw a 'chip butty' – something I had never come across before. Apparently my face was a picture of astonishment as I watched this 'starch on starch' meal being produced. I was never allowed to forget this and was ragged affectionately on many occasions about it. Fellow-prisoners also took delight in introducing me to many other aspects of life that I had never experienced before, but they always did it with humour. It said a lot that I was never laughed *at*, only *with*.

The diet was appalling with virtually no vitamin C. White bread was given to fill us up. Then one day some of us in the kitchen managed to get near enough to the visiting magistrates to ask for brown bread. I felt like Oliver Twist. But our request was granted, though the prison authorities did not seem amused that we had succeeded. Fruit was rationed to an apple a week, and this fact, coupled with our being locked in for long hours at a time, produced serious internal problems. I am still affected today, and suspect that most people who have experienced prison conditions will have piles or some other similar disorder.

The physical and emotional problems which we faced daily occupied a large part of our thinking – and this was without the added strain of being parted from our families or loved ones, and the knowledge of what they were going through on the outside.

Life could easily have become just a matter of survival; a fight to remain human and not be thought of as a number; a struggle to be the unique individuals we were. All this was rather like trying to swim with lead weights tied on to our feet. Some found it too difficult and painful, preferring to build

an impenetrable protective shell around their real
hurting, vulnerable selves.

How is it possible to live, not just exist, in such
an environment? The answer is: with the greatest
of difficulty. I realised how fortunate I was to have
been given the love and strength to keep going.
My own would have been totally inadequate. I
shuddered at the thought of even trying to cope
without God's love, very aware as I was of my
own weakness and vulnerability.

On bail I had grown accustomed to slipping into
the mid-week service in our church as well as on
Sundays. It had seemed a natural thing to do. Now,
thinking back to the last time I had tried to arrange
a service in Pucklechurch, I asked again if we
could have a communion service. 'Not possible
until September,' I was told. 'It is holiday time.'
So I prayed and waited for something that had
become my spiritual bread of life and felt should
not be denied us.

Only once in those three months was I able to receive communion. As before, it was a hurried affair
and I was left in no doubt as to the inconvenience
I was causing. There was seemingly no room in
Pucklechurch for Christ. However, he was there,
though unrecognised, longing to be used, to heal the
hurts and give love to the unloved.

On one occasion in our cell, Pat laughingly told
me to cool it. Many years later when we met again,
I reminded Pat of her remark at that time, and we
both laughed. Perhaps I was a little over the top, but
my only desire was to devote my life to the will of
God, regardless of the situation. After I had left for
Askham Grange, and she'd been sent to Durham, I

was thrilled and delighted to receive a letter from her saying that she was to be confirmed.

A great personal blow, as far as I was concerned, was the deliberate severing of communication with the outside world. This meant that I was unable to thank the people who had been so kind and wonderful to me on bail; nor could I write freely to those with whom I wanted to explore my faith, or share the joy that I had found in Christ. Letters were limited to two a week. Not to be able to correspond freely about spiritual matters was very distressing and frustrating. More and more I had to turn directly to God for my needs and feed only on him. Even so, deprived of communion and starved of spiritual correspondence, I felt indescribably lonely. David wrote occasionally, and I heard regularly from the convent where I had been on retreat, but I was seldom able to answer their letters, for if I wrote to them, I couldn't write to a family member that week.

I petitioned the Governor to be able to use my pocket money – 90p a week – to buy stamps instead of cigarettes and sweets, neither of which I needed. My request was denied. It seems to me that stopping contact between people through the written word is a cruel and unnecessary deprivation and I understood that other prisons did not have this rule.

By the end of September a place became available in Askham Grange, Yorkshire, and my stay in Pucklechurch came to an end. However, I am haunted to this day that Pucklechurch and its regime still exists.

# 7

# Open Prison

There is, in the last analysis, only one love, the love
that wells up eternally within God.

*Simon Tugwell*

I was surprised at the grandeur of Askham Grange
where I was to be for the rest of my sentence. As we
drove through the gates, I was full of apprehension,
for I knew that it was not the place that mattered so
much as the people in charge.

Those responsible for containing a variety of
individuals placed in it against their will, must
inevitably be aware of the mixture of pain, frustration and tension that will from time to time
break out. Askham was no exception, as I was to
find.

On arrival, after the usual reception procedure,
we were given a talk on a few ground rules and
issued with a cloth bag in which were a mug, knife,
fork and spoon. This time the cutlery was metal
but there was no sign of a teaspoon – something
which always intrigued me, for I could see no logical
reason why teaspoons were not issued. This meant,
as before, that when boiled eggs were produced,

they simply rolled around on a plate, and we ate them as best we could.

My bag was to stay with me at all times and as the months went by it became a hoard of small possessions! It seemed strange at first to be carrying around my cutlery, but I got used to it. I discovered that we were allowed to have our own mugs sent in and I was thrilled when Charlie proudly brought up for me one that he had chosen himself. It had on it the words: 'Presented to the World's Greatest Mum', and the picture of a mother wearing a hair-band, as I do, and a young girl and boy.

The mug survives still and is in daily use. Occasionally I tell people that it was my prison mug which I carried around in a cotton bag, clinking next to my cutlery and surrounded by letters, pencils and various treasures.

It was good to be eating off proper plates and not plastic ones. At the end of each meal, two buckets would be put on a table. In these we were expected to wash our mugs and cutlery before leaving the dining room. By the time seventy or eighty people had used the water it was none too clean, so if I was not among the first to leave I usually gave my utensils a good wash elsewhere.

Askham was an open prison but seemed to run on the principle of each for herself and the survival of the fittest. We were expected to keep our noses clean and little concern was shown for our physical or mental well-being. The only form of counselling that I could see was Alcoholics Anonymous, whose counsellors came in on a regular basis. I was saddened to discover that the majority of girls took tranquillisers to see them through their sentences. Many tried to sleep away their free time, except when receiving visits from family and friends. It was the only way they could cope.

The building itself put me in mind of a rather smart girls' boarding school. It was built in Tudor style, with lovely laid-out gardens, a duck pond, and a thriving walled market-garden. The surrounding fields and woods were idyllic, part of the beautiful village of Askham Richard. But even open prison does not mean the freedom to walk through any door. True, the doors are not locked but prisoners are expected to stay in the areas allocated to them both during working hours and in leisure time. There were constant checks to see that we complied, and roll calls before meals and at 9 p.m. From then on the night staff took over.

The emphasis was on manual work and I was assigned to the laundry, a dark room in the basement-cum-cellar, with no window, only a vent through which the steam from the washing machines could escape. An open gully ran behind the washing machines to take away the dirty water. Beside the machines, an area had been converted into showers. The water from these was also channelled into the gully. It was not uncommon for the drain to become blocked and then back-fill into the showers, thus flooding the whole area and giving off a permanent unpleasant smell. It was said that Askham Grange had been a hospital during the war and that the laundry area had been used as a morgue.

I recoiled in horror when I saw this place for the first time. Was I to spend my prison sentence among open drains in a dimly-lit laundry? Determined not to be beaten by the situation, I asked if I might attend the basic typing course in the education department as well as running the laundry. My request was refused at first, but I persisted and after several weeks I was given permission, on condition that the laundry work did not suffer. The education department was above ground level and at last I could look out of a window and see the sky during the day.

While on bail, I had discussed with David the possibility of putting my time to good use by broadening my education and gaining a good qualification, so that on my return to society, I might earn sufficient to support myself and my children. Until that point there had been no need for me to take a paid job. I planned to study Maths and French at O-Level and possibly English Literature at A-Level. But these plans were doomed to disappointment. I was told that O- and A-Level work wasn't considered necessary in Askham!

There was not even a proper library, as there is now, where I could at least have stretched my mind by reading. There were bookshelves on two of the walls of the television room, but the books had been there for years and were outdated. There was no affiliation with any library and no opportunity to order specific books.

Bitterly disappointed and needing the stimulus of study as an antidote to manual labour, I discussed the matter at length with the head of the education department, who eventually contacted York College to try and arrange for me to attend a course in French.

All this took several months and in the end, although I was interviewed by the French tutor, who provisionally agreed that the arrangements might be possible, the idea was turned down by the College because I was a prisoner. To give her due credit, the head of our prison education department pursued alternative courses and I was accepted in the business department. Why one department should discriminate against prisoners and another should not I shall never understand, but, at any rate, I was allowed to attend York College once a week, for their RSA course in shorthand and typing.

Although the shorthand classes were good, it is impossible to learn the skill without practice during the week and so, sadly, from that angle they were a waste of time. But walking the mile to and from the bus stop enabled me to be in the fresh air which was marvellous, even in the dark with the snow falling round me. One evening I missed the bus and walked the five miles into York.

Eventually a friend joined me on these trips which was a great relief, for it was difficult being the only one from prison, particularly when asked for one's phone number or invited out to coffee. To avoid such situations, the two of us tended to keep to ourselves even though this might have seemed anti-social to the others.

Much to my joy, I discovered a little chapel off the main hall, between the gym, which had obviously been a magnificent ballroom in its day, and the hospital and baby-unit wing. It was kept locked except when being used for services, but every Wednesday evening a mid-week Eucharist was held there. On Thursdays it was also used for informal 'songs of praise' services with the Methodist minister. It was

so good to sing and relax that I almost forgot I was in
a prison. We were also allowed to attend the Sunday
services at the local church in Askham Richard. It
was wonderful to be able to worship God again.

Letters were no longer limited, as long as we
bought the stamps out of the money we earned
– for me, this was £1.90 a week – and so I was
able to re-open, after three months' silence, my
correspondence with many people.

Receiving and writing letters was a more relaxed
matter at Askham. Unless there was some reason
for being given one privately, the incoming mail
was handed out to us at lunch-time. The names of
the lucky recipients were pinned up on a board or
called out. We then queued outside the dining-room
where an officer sat at a table with the post in front of
her. The envelopes were, of course, all slit open, but
unlike the system at Pucklechurch, only a few were
picked out at random and read through thoroughly.
The others were given a cursory inspection before
being handed to us. Any enclosures other than the
letters themselves were usually withheld until later
in the day so that they could be checked through
carefully. We were not supposed to have more than
twelve photographs in our possession at any one
time, though this rule was not strictly adhered to,
but none of the photographs were to include pictures
of ourselves. Anything we were not allowed was
locked away with our other belongings until our
release. Certain Christmas presents, magazines and
soap might be among such items.

I was so pleased at being able to correspond again
that not much else mattered to begin with. I quietly
went about my business, offering everything I did

and all those with whom I lived to God's love and mercy. Then something happened.

At the end of November, the Salvation Army approached the prison to ask for three people to cook lunch and tea for the elderly, lonely and housebound on Christmas Day, in their hall at Tadcaster. I was one of those chosen to go.

I still had very little idea of prison rules, but discovered that no one was allowed to go out or to receive visits on Christmas Day: a very poignant time of year, when feelings run high, and the pain of separation from loved ones can be overwhelming. Instead, prisons usually try to organise some form of Christmas celebration for all within their compounds, thus avoiding the friction likely to occur between those able to go out or be visited by families or friends and the rest.

A rumour began to circulate among the girls that I had been invited out to celebrate Christmas, because I happened to come from an upper-class background, was well off and influential! For some reason, the other two also chosen to help were not labelled in this way.

I was totally unaware of what was being spread around until one evening before tea when I wanted to spend five minutes in the chapel which had been opened for a Catholic service. As I walked into the hall, I came face to face with a sullen crowd. This was my first experience of being on the receiving end of mass resentment and anger and I was frightened.

A tall, strong, beautiful, coloured girl stepped forward and blocked my way. Intuitively, I grasped the situation. What the girl said wasn't important, it was the resentment and anger fuelling the crowd that was frightening. Judging that reason would fall on deaf ears just then, I simply said that what she had heard was not true, as I went to walk quietly through the crowd. It parted silently to let me through, then drew together again, like a sea wave. Strange though it may sound, I can only describe this as a kind of personal parting of the Red Sea!

On entering the chapel, I knelt in front of the altar with my heart pounding and my head full of confusion. I knew I had to speak to someone in case the situation should get out of hand completely. I prayed to God for help, then sought out the Catholic priest, whom I found in the hospital wing. Together we went back into the chapel and I poured out my fears. I felt that my relationship with my fellow-prisoners was much more important than anything that I had been asked to do on the outside, so I suggested giving up the idea of helping with the Salvation Army on Christmas Day, much as I would love to have been involved. Living with resentment and tension could prove destructive for all concerned; and it seemed only right and sensible to defuse the situation. We both agreed about this, so just before tea, I knocked on the head-of-staff's door and walked in. She was expecting me. She was so incredibly sensitive to all that was going on in the prison that she was aware of the rumours that were being spread about me and had anticipated that there might be some kind of reaction. She already appeared to know what I was about to ask. To my surprise, she refused my request to stay in Askham for Christmas. In fact, I was being ordered to go out! With a sinking heart I returned to the dining room, where everybody had already been checked in and was sitting down. I was reprimanded for being late: tea-times were used for roll calls to make sure no one had gone missing.

No one spoke to me; I had been sent to Coventry. Suddenly the head-of-staff entered the dining room and there was a silence. She spoke about the work we would be doing on Christmas Day, making it clear that this entailed our missing out on everything planned for the others. You could have heard a pin drop as she explained the situation and thus helped to clear the air a little, but some were still convinced that I was being favoured, and continued their policy of non-communication.

It was in the dark, dank laundry, from which I had recoiled, that the situation was resolved. The next day, the girl who had spoken to me came down there on her own. Looking up and seeing a face full of frustration and resentment, I suddenly ceased to be afraid and found myself loving her instead. She threw her personal laundry on the ground for me to do, although each prisoner was expected to wash the clothes she wore. My job was to wash the kitchen laundry, such as tea-cloths and overalls, towels from various parts of the prison, table cloths and sundries from the staff building adjacent to the prison.

Gently I shook the girl by the shoulders and asked her to explain what was 'bugging' her. What came out was so distorted, but so full of her own hurt, that I was near to tears. I also saw how the resentment had arisen: she had been invited by her prison visitor to go out and spend Christmas Day with her, but naturally her request to be allowed to do this had been turned down. The story that had circulated about me had thus been like a red rag to a bull.

Aware of my own tendency to assume things about people or situations, I sympathised with how this girl and the others had felt. By opening up to each other, we found ourselves standing on common ground, and this was to be the beginning of a wonderful relationship. I taught her to play chess and, with her quick mind, she soon outstripped me. I couldn't keep pace with her physically except in swimming, for there were twenty years between us to her advantage, but I was never far behind as we ran and worked out in the gym together. I surprised myself and, I think, others by my ability to keep up. We spent long hours discussing the philosophy of life from such different angles that it was quite fascinating.

What happened between us affected the others. When they, too, realised the truth, and saw that I was not a creature from another planet, but as human and vulnerable as everyone else, they gradually came to talk to me openly about themselves. I was appalled by the tragedies that were revealed, and recognised, in the hot, smelly laundry, how fortunate I was to receive these confidences and be able to share the love that God had given me.

I heard much later, from an outside source, that it was thought that I would not survive Askham, and that, sooner or later, I would have to be moved to a closed prison for my own protection. I am glad that those who believed this were proved wrong.

I learned to love the laundry, despite its lack of fresh air, for it had given me something beyond price; the chance to be with others in distress.

Our trust in one another was something I found very affirming.

I often pondered over some of the restrictions of Askham Grange. Diaries and playing cards were forbidden. It seemed a pity about the cards and I couldn't understand why diaries weren't permitted. I understand that both are now allowed. At the time I felt I needed the equivalent of a diary if only for making notes of visiting days, letters written and any specific events that I might wish to remember. I had requested and been permitted to have an appeal book for recording correspondence with my solicitor. I had only found out through talking with another inmate that this type of book would be authorised; such matters were left unsaid by the staff. Having got the book, I decided to use the last five pages as a secret diary. As I shaded off each day, I could think that I was one day nearer to being reunited with the children.

On the day I had been sentenced, the defence felt that we should try and submit my case to the Appeal Court in London – a procedure open to all who feel there is a possibility that their sentence may be reduced. If the Court of Appeal accepts the case, a date is fixed for the hearing. My defence counsel felt that though our chance of success was slim, it was worth a try. My appeal was due to be heard on December 6th. We were driven to the London Appeal Court by a Yorkshire taxi-driver, who lost his way, so we didn't arrive in time. As a result we were late, and my case was deferred to the end of the day. Then, after all that waiting, the appeal was dismissed and, broken-hearted, I was driven back to Askham.

I was taken aback by the kindness I received on my return. One girl gave me the flowers given to her by her boyfriend. Yet others gave cards. I was supported and carried by this love and understanding from people who, knowing what it was like to be hurt, wanted to help a fellow-sufferer.

As the weeks before Christmas drew near, a list was put up for those who wanted to go carol singing round the village. Although I put my name on the list, I was not allowed to go – for reasons which mystified me. I got the impression that the staff felt that I didn't need the same help and opportunities as the other girls, who fortunately were by now well aware that I was just as vulnerable as they were.

One day my father rang to say that my mother had had a heart attack, was very weak and temporarily paralysed down one side. He was very distressed and asked whether I could get parole and come and see her. Normally girls were allowed home for a couple of days in such situations. Desperately upset, knowing that the strain of all that I had put my parents through had played a considerable part in my mother's failing health, I made an application to the Governor to go home for a night. He bluntly asked me if my mother was going to die. I was so taken aback and stunned that I said I did not know. 'In that case,' he said, 'your application is refused.'

The girls were horrified at his decision, and without their support I do not know how I could have managed. I found it very hard to be treated by the staff as though I were somehow different from everyone else. If they were under the impression that I could cope with anything, they had grossly misjudged me. Unfortunately, this decision greatly affected my parents as well as myself, for they really needed me at that time. The prison staff's attitude was a hurt in itself with which I had to come to terms, while being unable to see the logic behind some of the decisions they made concerning me.

Christmas Day arrived and I spent it as arranged with the Salvation Army in Tadcaster. The work was hard, but so transformed by love and joy that we never noticed it. We cooked lunch. Then, while the other two were serving it to those gathered in the Salvation Army hall, another person and I went out to take Christmas lunch to some of those who were housebound. It was one of the most poignant Christmas Days I have ever experienced. If I had not been in prison, I would never have found myself in the position of abandoning the family on Christmas Day in order to help others in this way. It was such a pleasure to listen to, share a smile and laugh with those I met. We called round again in the afternoon, with Christmas cake and a present for each person. My heart was full that day and I received a hundred times more than I gave.

After tea was served in the hall, we sang songs of praise, carols and hymns, and listened to some Bible readings. The three of us were asked to sing to the guests. Not one of those invited knew that we were prisoners from Askham Grange. Among the requests was 'Amazing Grace'. I have never sung that song before with such a bursting heart. It was 9 p.m. when we returned to the prison, each of us having received a very precious gift – that of seeing God's love in action.

We had evidently been such a good team, and

had gone down so well with the elderly, that the Salvation Army asked us to help with their next large event. The answer from the authorities was no, since opportunities like this were considered privileges to be shared among other prisoners too. I tried to explain this to a rather puzzled woman from the Salvation Army who had come in for a service in the chapel and happened to see me in the corridor, and to emphasise how much I should have wanted to help if this had been possible.

In Askham I had started off sleeping in a dormitory with four other girls, but eventually I was asked if I would share a little two-bedded room near the attic. It was a difficult decision, because although being there would give me a little more privacy, the room only had a skylight window, from which it was impossible to see out, and this gave me a sense of claustrophobia. Nevertheless, I decided to move.

Early one evening, watching the clouds scudding across the sky in a stiff breeze, I longed to be outside in the fresh air. I pictured myself and Ben, my golden retriever, roaming free over the fields near home, and the feeling of claustrophobia became too much. I propped a chair against the sloping wall and climbed up. Balancing precariously, I could just see out into the fields. It was getting dark; the trees were silhouetted against the sky and I looked longingly out. On an impulse I went downstairs to the office and before I could stop myself, blurted out, 'Please may I go outside for five minutes? I need the fresh air.' It was a silly request, and I knew before I asked what the answer would be. I was given a strange look and told where to put myself!

Despite the daily tedium, there were lighter moments and laughs. We were responsible for cleaning our own rooms and very often there were spot-checks to see if any dust could be found there. One day I returned to find a note on my bed. I had failed to wipe the dust off the leaves of my cyclamen plant. I found this unbelievable and decided there was only one suitable response.

I wrote a grateful ode from the plant to the officer who had left the cryptic message and propped it up against the pot for her to find the next day. The poem disappeared, so I hope she enjoyed reading it as much as I enjoyed writing it!

In early summer I was moved from the laundry to work as education orderly. This meant, among other things, keeping the classrooms clean and typing out the weekly notices for evening classes. One morning I was looking out of the window when I noticed a horse wandering in through the gates. Without hesitating, I ran downstairs intending to catch and return it to its owner, who lived down the road. I stripped off my jersey, thinking to use it as a makeshift rope. Unfortunately, by the time I reached the garden, the horse, thoroughly frightened by an irate gardener, tore past me and out on to the road. To my relief, it was soon caught. I was highly amused on my return to the education department to hear that all sorts of rumours were flying around, including one about how I had leapt on to the back of a wild animal. Someone even asked me if I was related to Joy Adamson!

I had been in Askham several months when a spate

of fires broke out in our rooms. We had an arsonist in our midst but, try as they might, the authorities were unable to discover the culprit. One evening at about 9 p.m., I was downstairs playing chess with a friend when the fire alarm went off again. We all evacuated the building, as on previous occasions, but then, with a sense of shock, I saw flames and smoke pouring out of the skylight of our bedroom. It didn't take much imagination to recognise the seriousness of the situation, for if the fire had spread to the rafters, the whole roof would have been in danger.

Fortunately, the fire was soon under control and then extinguished. For several nights after that, while investigations were going on, our room remained padlocked. I was not allowed in to see if any books or clothing remained, and had to live with borrowed nightwear and the clothes I had on my back. My room-mate was about to go on home leave the next day, prior to being released. Luckily the clothes she needed for her visit had been collected, checked, and were being held in reception till the morning.

Eventually, after the investigation, I was told to scrub out the room and make it habitable. As I opened the door, I was faced with blackened charred remains and an acrid smell that caught in my throat. My bed was totally destroyed and the other one partially so. Many of my clothes were burnt but, to my utter amazement, at the end of my bed, on top of the scorched and blistered locker, my Bible and spiritual books had remained completely untouched. They were damp, but unmarked by the fire. I was unable to claim damages for clothes, as everything we owned was there at our own risk. However, the prison tried hard to help me, and replaced what I had lost as best they could from their own stocks.

The task of cleaning up the mess single-handed was daunting, but I need not have worried. Two people gave up all their free time to help me scrub the place out. These two had more to be bitter about than most of the others, for they were lifers. It took us all weekend and a little more to finish the job. It was backbreaking work, but my two helpers stuck at it with me.

I found many such examples of helpfulness and generosity in prison. People were very ready to share what little they had, whether possessions, time, or themselves. Certainly, I was never short of real loving support. Touched but horrified, I learned that one girl, believing me to be in my bedroom at the time of the fire, had raced up the stairs to help me. I still feel sick at the thought of what might have happened to her.

Maybe it was this love, this kindness in people whom society had in some cases rejected when they needed help, and then condemned, that opened my eyes to the flame of love in each one of us.

Despite the support from my friends around me, there were still times when I experienced utter loneliness and desolation. I craved for someone with whom to share the deep longings of my heart and soul. In fact I became quite desperate, and in the end I smuggled out a note to the rector of the local parishes. It was strange how the opportunity arose. The boiler flue in the little church outside the gates had become blocked with a bird's nest, causing a fire. As a result, although no structural damage had been done, the whole of the inside of the church was black with smoke and fumes. After cleaning and redecorating the walls, volunteers were asked for from Askham Grange prison to scrub and rewax the pews.

I was one of the volunteers, and I tucked a note inside my clothing on the off-chance that the vicar might come over to see how the cleaning was progressing. I prayed that I wouldn't be searched on the way out, and my prayers were answered. The second hurdle was more difficult, for a couple of officers were with us all the time. The vicar did come in to see us, and however astonished he might have been, his expression never altered as I brushed past him, thrusting my note into his hand.

It was soon after this that he made arrangements with the Governor to come in and see me on a regular basis.

It was truly wonderful to be able to sit with him in the chapel, deep in conversation on a level that would otherwise have been impossible, about theology, worship and prayer. He gave me the spiritual support, guidance and companionship which I needed so much. Being aware of my weaknesses, I turned to him for confession. I also needed to be kept from pursuing my own private religious path, and he was very good at bringing me down to earth!

He made sure that if the Sunday service in Askham Richard did not include communion, those of us who wanted to go would be able to attend church in one of his other parishes. Either a mini-bus from the prison would escort us, for we needed parole licences to attend outside the village, or we were taken privately to the relevant parish. He began to ask me and a friend of mine to read the lessons and Gospels in three of his parishes until I actually began to feel part of the outside community; to have a sense of belonging in my own right as a person, not as a prisoner.

At our Thursday evening services of prayer and praise in our own little chapel, the organist from Askham Richard came in and played the piano for us. She was a lovely person who always had a ready smile. Soon after I arrived the matter of a choir was raised. The organist said that there originally had been one from the prison, but this had dwindled and ceased. However, she agreed to explore the possibility of starting something up again. To my joy she did, and six of us became the new choir. We practised the hymns each Thursday after the service. I thanked God for the opportunities that were opening up not just for me but also for all of us who wished to turn to Christ.

My prison visitor, who was a Methodist, usually attended our Thursday evening services, and often invited me to his church too. I was able to go, as these services were nearly always held on a Sunday evening. I looked forward to all the services. They were the times when I was able to shed, for a little while, the pain of being parted from the children and my parents, and to worship God; when through his love I was renewed and given the strength I needed to live out my time in prison, a prospect which sat like a great burden on my shoulders.

The mother and baby unit at Askham, in the same wing as the hospital, was out of bounds to all who were not directly involved with it. At the age of two, children would be parted from their mothers and sent out to live with relatives. The pain caused by this abrupt, early severing of the bond between mother and child must have been indescribable. I wondered what would happen to babies who had no relatives able to take over.

If I had a spare moment I would help take the babies out for walks, particularly on a Saturday morning. Although the unit was in the same building, for Askham Grange was a massive house, the babies were not allowed into the rest of the prison, except when they were taken into the gym to play and listen to music. I was amazed to discover that mothers worked in other parts of the prison, rather than looking after their own babies. Girls from our side of the prison were given that job. Surely, the opportunity should have been seized not only to allow mothers to care for their young but also to teach them more about family responsibilities and relationships. However I gathered from some mothers that they preferred to work, as this enabled them to have a break from their babies and mix with the other prisoners.

Warned by one of the girls on my first day, not to be ill, I was then regaled with some gruesome horror stories. Unfortunately being locked up in Pucklechurch for hours on end had taken its toll and one day, in great discomfort I found it necessary to report to the surgery. It did not take me long to understand the girl's warning. I was dealt with for piles under local anaesthetic, stitched up and sent straight back to work. I was in considerable pain when the anaesthetic wore off, and could hardly climb back up the stairs from the laundry at the end of the day. My personal experience in this matter was by no means exceptional.

We were extremely vulnerable to the moods of the staff. Some I could trust, others I stayed clear of if at all possible. On one occasion, as an extra duty, I was asked to wash the long ground-floor corridor. Having finished this, I was about to put away my bucket and mop when one of the staff walked up. For some reason best known to herself, she wanted to see me on my hands and knees, and ordered me to do the job again with a scrubbing brush. She waited with an expression of satisfaction on her face until I complied. Only when I was down on my knees, did she walk away.

She might have been surprised and disconcerted if she had been able to read the thoughts running through my head as I worked, for I had decided to offer every sweep of the scrubbing brush as a prayer – and I found myself including her in my prayers. I couldn't resist chuckling as I tried to visualise how she would feel about this! It proved to be a marvellous way of cleaning the corridor and removing all feelings of personal degradation. I finished the job with a stiff back but a light heart.

Another time I had a larger than usual load of laundry and was unable to book in by 12 noon on the Saturday to attend Sunday church. In fact I was five minutes late. This same member of staff stood there forbidding me to add my name to the list. She knew what missing church would mean to me. It was a useless threat, for nothing on this earth would have stopped me attending. I would have broken parole and taken the consequences. After lunch one of the staff who had been writing out the list, told me that she had quietly added my name to it: I think she understood the lengths to which I would go and the outcry that would follow if I hadn't been allowed to go to chu:ch.

I found it quite astonishing that anyone in charge, with complete authority over another human being, could be so deliberately vindictive; the conclusion I came to was that a deep inner hurt must be driving her to kick out at someone completely at her mercy.

It was the lighter moments, rather than such things, about which I wrote to my family and friends. I described incidents to make them laugh and think that I was all right; for how could I add to their pain by burdening them with mine? Only David knew some of my agony and guessed the rest; he understood all that I didn't say. He was wonderful too in the way he answered my questions whenever possible, encouraging me when I was low, giving me good advice and snippets of local news.

On the whole, life revolved around visits: from children, relatives and friends. It seemed an eternity before I saw the children two months later at the end of October. It was not thought possible to bring them up often, but when I saw the other children visiting their mothers every fortnight, it was very difficult to accept that decision. It caused me so much distress that I talked this through with the prison probation service, who were sympathetic. They were well aware that, contrary to what most people think, the less children see of their imprisoned parents, the more traumatic and painful each visit becomes. After moving from Pucklechurch to Askham Grange, I saw Victoria only three times. A few years later, when the children and I were able to talk about these things, Victoria confirmed that she had felt the need to see me more often.

Visiting took place in our canteen-cum-dining hall. We were placed at tables allocated to us. We were not allowed to rise or move from our places, although our visitors could buy us drinks and sweets from the canteen counter. After visiting was over, we were called up, one by one, and taken to a small room where we were searched before we were free to go. We learned to accept this as a matter of routine.

On the children's first visit, the waiting had been too much for me. Powerless to stop myself, I leapt to my feet and ran towards them. Victoria did the same and we met in the middle of the room, and then stood, arms around each other crying. The whole canteen fell silent – not a dry eye in the place. I suddenly realised what I had done and we quietly went and sat down. For once I was not rebuked.

It was agony not being at home with the children, unable to help them when they needed me. My heart bled for them when they got into any sort of trouble, and I longed to comfort them, knowing that often they were simply reacting to the fact that I was in prison.

The experience of being forced to let go of the children is not one that I would wish on anybody. Letting them go gradually, as and when they are ready for it, so that they can grow up, become independent and mature, is difficult but right. But to have to let go abruptly when they are still very vulnerable and need parenting, is another matter altogether. It is impossible to know the extent of the damage done by experiences like these and the hurt that may erupt at a later stage in some form or other. If one has been the unwilling cause of such pain, this is indeed hard to bear! Each time the children visited me, the knowledge that I could do so little for them hit me like a hammer blow. Silently I would offer up my burden to God; a burden carried by many other women around me in prison.

My family were very good, making sure that there was always someone to visit me. It cannot have been easy for them, but they never let me down.

There is no doubt that I was given immense support through postcards and letters from many people who always kept in touch even though I was unable to answer every letter immediately. I was aware of their concern, their love and prayers. What they gave was beyond price.

There was the joy, in an open prison, of going out walking on a Saturday or Sunday through the beautiful woods and lanes. Just being able to walk, listen to the birds, absorb the beauty, was like a healing touch from God.

During my stay in Askham, the recreational activities were improved out of all proportion. Some weekends, instead of going for walks, we were taken round the walls of York, or given a tour of the great cathedral. The last time I visited it was just before it was struck by lightning. Running and orienteering were added to the activities, and I participated as much as I was able to, revelling in the fresh air after the enclosed environment of the laundry all week.

I ran in a mini-marathon for charity round York race-course, something I would not have dreamed of doing previously; and on receiving a certificate for swimming 2,000 metres, I laughed as I recalled happier times.

Orienteering, a sport which had become very popular, was usually held on Sundays, and after an early lunch several of us were allowed to participate in competitions, if they were within an hour's driving distance. We all went dressed in the bright yellow waterproof jackets issued to those who tended the garden. They were very practical and the colour was easy to see which was useful if any of us got lost.

One particular afternoon, one of us accidentally dropped a slip of paper which told her to report to the office for some minor misdemeanour – and had 'Askham Grange' written on it! Someone behind the girl with the slip saw it fall, retrieved it, and later handed it in to the administration tent, where there was a little explaining to do, since we had let it be known that we had come from a rather exclusive boarding school! From then on we were always careful to search our pockets before leaving the prison.

Life in prison was very much like a boarding school at times. On the evening before a person was released, the poor unfortunate girl was fair game, and we would plan all sorts of school-girl pranks. There was always an unwritten boundary over which we never stepped, but we went fairly close one evening when we bound a poor girl in a sheet and left her on a forbidden landing to be found by the night staff. She put up a terrible struggle and, giving me a mournful look, said, 'Not you

too, Jenny!' as I tied an extra-secure knot to stop
her escaping. I felt quite guilty.

Every year we performed a pantomime, and this
year it was The Grand Old Duke of York. By general
consensus I was picked to play the Grand Old Duke
himself. We gave one evening over to handicapped
children. To see their faces light up, to bring them
on to the stage, dance, sing and laugh with them,
was so wonderful that tears of joy still come to my
eyes when I remember it.

In a strange way, Askham had become my home, for
I could no more love and live in a vacuum than fly.
My lifestyle had changed dramatically, but I tried
to make the most of everything possible as I shared
in the lives of those around me. This had opened
my eyes as nothing else could have done. As has
been rightly said: Experience is the best teacher.
I would certainly add that some things can only be
learnt properly through experience.

One very special memory will stay with me for
ever. A group of girls had been chosen to go on an
outward bound weekend on the Yorkshire moors.
All in their early twenties and physically very fit, they
were a group who, it was felt, would benefit from the
experience. One of the girls chosen to go suffered
from bouts of depression which made her rather
unpredictable, and the only reason I was allowed
to go along with them, was to help with her should
the need arise.

Our base was the Outward Bound school at
Barnard Castle. The school, along with an Outward
Bound instructor, was entirely given over to us for
the duration. On our first evening, we were given

lectures on how to read a map, use a compass, pack and carry rucksacks, and what to do if we got lost! Then came supper, cooked by us, and bed. Up early the next morning we started with a two-mile run before breakfast, followed by canoeing on the river – something I had not done before – then, with tents and all our equipment on our backs, we set off for the Yorkshire moors. We climbed higher and higher, through a drizzle first of all and then driving rain. We must have looked a sodden bedraggled lot as we made our stumbling, exhausted way up the slopes. But eventually the downpour ended and, as we reached our destination, the sky cleared and the soft evening light bathed the moors. They drew me by their beauty and their promise of solitude.

After we had put up the tents, and eaten a meal, I had a great urge to be alone to pray, there in the type of countryside I loved the most. So, impulsively I asked the instructor from the Outward Bound school if I could go for a walk. He never gave it a second thought and, after checking that I knew what to do if I got lost, let me go.

I had not gone far when I heard, floating through the still air, a conversation.

'Where's Jenny?' came the voice of the prison warden.

'Gone for a walk,' the instructor's voice answered.

'Gone for a what?'

'A walk.'

'She can't do that, she's a prisoner!' The warden's voice sounded a little disturbed.

'She's O.K. She needed to be alone,' I heard the instructor say.

I walked on and the voices faded. I felt rather sorry for the prison warden, but I was not going to spoil this very special moment, for I was free, I was alone, I had privacy, I was with God.

As dusk stole over the moors, the sky deepened its blue and the evening star shone out. Even the broken dry-stone wall I leaned on became alive with beauty. The Yorkshire moors had turned into the biggest cathedral in the world. I looked up, and saw no limit to its height. All creation sang in hymns of praise and glory. As I stood alone, for the first time for a year, tears of joy and love rolled down my cheeks and I stretched out my arms to join in creation's song.

'Pee-wit, pee-wit,' sang the plover, and the sound echoed over the barren moor, then faded away.

As more stars appeared, I knew that the time had come for me to return. A couple of rabbits were playing on the slope opposite me. I walked back along the side of a stream, which sang and danced its way down the hill, and my heart danced with it.

As I neared the small cluster of tents, I could hear the murmuring of sleepy voices. It seemed ridiculous to think that out here in the open, curled up in their sleeping bags, were a group of prisoners. I joined my two friends in our tent and crawled into my sleeping bag for the night.

God had given me a precious moment in time that I would never forget. I saw with the utmost clarity that all of us, whether in prison or free, whether rejected by society or not, are often in prisons of our own making; and that only God can bring us real freedom. He is our hope and salvation. When we recognise and give ourselves to him, he holds us in his strength and love. He makes the impossible possible, rekindling his flame within us, and he alone has the right to be our judge.

Snuggled in my sleeping bag, I could still feel the cool night air on my face, with the memory of that walk fresh in my mind. Out there, on the moors, it had all been so special that I had longed for time to stop. But none of us can stay in a rarefied atmosphere. It had only been a small glimpse of God's glory from which I had to return to ordinary living, having been made richer and stronger by the experience.

Soon after this, I was granted parole. I had spent fifteen months of my two years in prison. I was free to return and start my life again, but only under the supervision of the probation service until my two years were up. My parents drove up to Askham Grange for the last time to collect me. I had offered every day of my sentence to Christ, and knew I had been held by his love through every moment. He had been there beside me, through my pain and my tears: my rock and my salvation.

It was strange leaving the place which I felt had become my home. With my heart and mind full of the precious glimpses that people had given me into their lives, I was to find it almost impossible to concentrate on the general conversation of ordinary life. The life that I was about to return to was far removed from the life that I had led over the past year. I had the greatest difficulty in leaving behind all those I had grown to love. It would feel strange not being able to pop into the little chapel that I now knew so well. I would miss it, I thought, realising again what an oasis it had been for me.

I revisited this chapel recently and was thrilled to discover that it is now open all day for anyone to enter at any time. I saw spiritual books on the shelves, comfortable chairs in the corner. It had become a place where one could be alone, to cry out one's grief in privacy; to pray; to experience the love of God and grow within that love; a place to discover one's own worth in his eyes. There was even a box of tissues lying on a table to mop up any tears before leaving the chapel! This haven of privacy had not been available during my time at Askham.

Through my relationship with God and through seeing and sharing in the lives of those less fortunate than myself, my concerns had changed radically. For one thing, I was now more aware of people suffering in all kinds of ways, anywhere in the world.

At the same time that I was in prison, people in the Sudan were suffering from the most terrible famine and starving to death in their hundreds. Although we had enough to eat, our diet was pretty poor, and at one point everyone decided to go on a hunger strike in protest. I felt pulled apart – for the problem in our prison was real, but at least we were not dying for lack of food. Vivid pictures came to my mind of the poverty which I had seen in India as a young child, and in Hong Kong in my early twenties. As a result, I was able to imagine quite easily the tragedy that the people of the Sudan were facing on such a large scale. Coming to terms with the two problems was so difficult, that I found myself putting it on paper in the form of poetry, as I tried to explain what was in my heart. Since then, I have continued to express my views and feelings in that medium, and now have a small collection of poems.

I tried to discuss with my parents the issues which had faced me in prison. I had been forced to rethink everything. Questions to which I had given little thought before now filled my mind. What were prisons all about? What effect did they have on people? What constructive changes should be made to take into account rehabilitation, so that people could integrate back into the community unashamed, and as responsible citizens? Was the system really conducive to deterring and reforming people? I felt a lot of very serious questions needed answering.

At the same time I was having to rethink my own identity and purpose in the light of my new experience of God, and the issues that this threw up.

I realised I was on foreign ground as far as my parents were concerned. Too much had happened in those fifteen months' separation. All they wanted to do was to welcome me home. They had waited so long for my return and had supported me loyally and lovingly throughout my ordeal. Now they only wanted to share in putting us together as a family. My thoughts would only hurt and puzzle them. What they needed from me, and what I wanted so desperately to share with them, were incompatible.

My family and children were still of the greatest importance to me, but through offering myself to the service of Christ, the balance of my values had changed: family life was not now the only priority. I could not turn my back on all that I had been allowed to see and experience, for it had become part of me.

In effect, prison was to make me a double outcast. God had become the centre of my reality, so I no longer fitted into my previous life, and socially many found me unacceptable. It is painful to be an outcast, and there were really dark days and nights as I struggled with my dilemma. But since Christ had carried me through prison, I knew he would carry me through the rest of my life.

As I drove away from Askham Grange that morning, I accepted that life was not going to be easy, but that, through God's love and the love of my family and friends, all things would be well in the end.

# 8

# Aftermath

If we imagine ourselves to be in the hands of God as clay is in the hands of the potter, then we can see desolation as a turning of the clay so that it becomes a vessel which can contain life-giving water which as unformed clay it could not hold.

*Gerard W. Hughes*

Every ex-offender has to face rejection in one form or another. As my parents and I travelled home together on that first day of my release, I was aware of this at the back of my mind but rather naïvely thought it would not affect me too much. But, as I was soon to discover, being aware of something and actually experiencing it, are entirely different matters. Besides, my thoughts were rather more on the people left behind in Askham Grange. It seemed clear to me that improvements were necessary and possible in the system. I prayed that God would open the eyes of those in charge so that constructive alternatives to some of the current practices could be found and implemented.

Something else that I was soon to learn was that, as a side-effect of my being in prison, I had become institutionalised. As a child, decisions had been made for me and I had accepted school rules and regulations as part of the life of an institution. As I grew up and was given more responsibility, I learned to make my own decisions. This is all part of maturing into an adult. Put an adult back into a situation where all decisions are removed, and very soon the process is reversed, until the ability to make sound decisions and judgments is lost. I feel that if it is at all possible in prisons, ways should be found to give real responsibilities to inmates long before they leave prison, thereby taking a valuable step towards rehabilitation.

The combination of rejection and institutionalisation soon hit me with full force on my return to society. It would be easy to assume that when I walked out of prison and was reunited with my family, I should be filled with joy, but such was not the case. To make normal decisions concerning everyday living, particularly as a single parent, became a task that I found quite daunting, and the months that followed my release were difficult and stressful. I was sustained by the knowledge that I was being held in love and prayer, and this awareness literally carried me through the following months.

In prison I had not been able to attend Christopher's funeral or given space to grieve over his death. Though not really aware of it, I was still talking about Christopher as present. My logic told me this could not be so, but my heart had not been given the chance to come to terms with his death. One of my new-found friends had the courage to point this out to me, and through the love and support from her and others I learned to live with the reality of the situation.

Sadly some friends who had cared for me and helped me before I went to prison, didn't know how to accept me now. I realised that the situation had become awkward, and that it would be far easier for them to fade into the background. However, a handful of widely-scattered friends were very supportive.

Although it was wonderful to be together with my family again, all my energies were concentrated on trying to put together a stable home for them. I know that without their trust in me, and without the support I was being given by my parents, brothers, sister and friends, I should have crumbled. Life after prison was anything but a bed of roses. I slept fitfully, having got used to the hourly checks at night in prison, and often woke up sobbing. Many times in the succeeding weeks, I was to wake to the sound of my own voice crying, 'Abba, Father!' It was a desperate call to God to make things well.

I had returned to temporary rented accommodation and, as the children were still at boarding school, took the opportunity to go into retreat for five days. I remember the addresses were based on the beatitudes. When I got back I found I had been burgled. The thieves had been quite thorough, and had had time to take all they wanted. I was uninsured, for I was living on social benefits, with insurance low on my list of priorities. Among the things taken were items of sentimental value to me, and the children's christening presents. Though sad about this, I couldn't help smiling at the same time, for my mind was still on the beatitudes, in the light of which the burglary didn't seem that important.

For the next couple of years my parents supported me with their love, and we became very close. They lived only a few miles away, and we were able to see each other often. Financially I was having the most tremendous struggle, and I experienced what it was like to try and bring up a family relying on Social Security benefits. Until I could stand on my own feet with a proper job, friends, family and those in the local community made sure we always had enough to eat. A Christian charity also helped me to clothe the children. Having been brought up by the maxim that it is better to give than to receive, it was very hard at first to learn to receive. However, sensing the joy it gave to those doing the giving, and being in the position of *having* to receive, put the whole thing in perspective. It made me realise that as long as the giving and receiving is done with unconditional love, it is immaterial who is the giver and who is the receiver.

Despite the love I was being given, I became very depressed, and sought my doctor's advice. For a short while I was put back on anti-depressants and sleeping pills. It was now the summer holidays, and the feeling of being quite worthless and useless lay heavy on my heart. But the Mothers' Union had not forgotten me. Barely a month after my release, I was asked to help run one of their holidays on the Isle of Wight for a hundred people. It was exactly what I needed to give me back a sense of my self-worth and also proved to be a marvellous place for children. The large house was on the edge of the cliff overlooking a wonderful bay. There was a path down to the sandy beach, with no road to cross. The house had a little chapel which we used every morning for a time of informal prayer in which someone offered a thought for the day. I was thrilled when asked to lead one of these morning reflections. To be able to offer something that might touch a person's heart with God's love, was a privilege, and it felt so right to be there. The fact that the chapel was so much a normal part of the house, with a wonderful informal atmosphere, encouraged both adults and children to come in freely, and more and more attended the morning and evening prayers as the week progressed.

I shall never forget that week which gave me so much. It was as though the whole holiday was wrapped in God's love. People gradually began to smile and look relaxed. Helpers and holiday-makers alike came away feeling that we had experienced something special. Feeling needed, wanted, useful and normal was particularly important to me after having lived as a number for so long. My children loved it there, and Victoria later asked if she could go back and help when she was a little older.

What struck me at the time was that the Mothers' Union hadn't looked on me as someone different, either to pity, help or scorn, but as a person of value to be used. I found it extraordinary to reflect on the fact that it was the little prayer book from the Mothers' Union that had spoken to me in prison, sowing the very first seeds of faith. In a sense I owe my faith to them. Their prime concern is the support and strengthening of marriage and family life. Having been helped so much by them, I wanted to be part of what they were doing and so became a member.

On our return from that holiday there were two immediate things to do. The first was to find a home for the children and myself where we could put down roots and start rebuilding our family again, and the second, to find employment. I decided to buy a house in the same area where we had lived previously, and this we did. I wanted the children to be able to live openly and honestly, without having to invent lies to cover up what had happened. This would be possible there. As for me, I put myself entirely into God's hands, praying that he would continue to hold us in his love whatever the situation. Gone was our big house with tennis court, large cars and parties. Gone too was the falsely glamorous life that I had led before. Instead I was entering a life of reality, a life where God was present in the ordinary events of daily living. My solicitor had managed to hang on to enough money from the sale of our old house, which had taken place while I had been in prison, for us to have a sweet little semi-detached house on an estate. We had a home; I was with my children; my parents lived not far away; and we had love, that precious gift which I had discovered in prison.

I shall never forget the day we moved in. Two of my new neighbours discovered that I had just been released from prison and slipped a note through the door before my arrival, welcoming me to the estate. To prevent any embarrassing explanations by me, the note also said that they knew I had been in prison. I was very moved, particularly as it didn't stop there. Hot sustaining soup and rolls were brought in, as we worked to put the house in order.

Being back in a house of our own gave me a sense of freedom and security that was particularly valuable at this time. Except for reporting to the probation office – usually a condition of any early release – I was not beholden to anyone. I began to stand on my own feet.

I walked into the town and I found a welcome there, too, in every shop that I entered. It was very moving, and I knew that whatever was to come, I had made the right decision about where we should live.

My next priority was employment. I discovered that although I had done a typing course in prison, it was not one that was recognised by employment agencies, and therefore I did not have sufficient qualifications to apply for a secretarial position. But the greatest shock was discovering that with a prison record, no one was keen to put me on their books. One agency said it was not their policy to employ people from prison. I realised then that punishment didn't stop on release from prison. In effect, the sentence begins again but with a different approach. Through discussions with ex-offenders I have again and again come across this problem of employers being reluctant to take on a person from prison.

The whole thing can become a vicious circle. If ex-offenders are turned down as a result of telling the truth, they are likely to lie or keep silent about their past next time they are seeking employment. (On occasion I have been reduced to keeping silent or failing to fill in the relevant part of an application form.) If they are subsequently found out, they are blamed and possibly sacked for their dishonesty. Without a job, rejected by society, they feel bitter and hopeless. All this encourages them to turn back to crime.

Not to be beaten by the stigma of prison, I enrolled at our nearest technical college for a recognised secretarial course, after which I worked for six months in the secretarial department of a drug addiction centre on a voluntary basis, until I felt I had sufficient experience to apply for a salaried job.

Just when I was beginning to feel better in myself, a phone call came through from Bath saying that my father had died of a heart attack and the shock of this had proved too great for my mother who had also collapsed. I arrived to find them both dead. Stunned though I was, I knelt beside my mother's bed, where she had collapsed, and prayed for them both. As I offered them to God, I gave thanks that neither had been left to grieve for the other. They had gone together. However, I felt as though the carpet had been pulled from underneath my feet. My brothers arrived soon afterwards, having had further to drive, so we were able to make the necessary arrangements together. We wired my sister in Australia, who flew in on the next available plane.

Because the double death was so unusual, the press got on to it, and unfortunately discovered that I had been in prison. They rang to say they were printing the story but, just in time, our solicitor was able to stop them. I couldn't believe that a reporter could be so insensitive at such a distressing moment for us all. It was the first time since Christopher's death that I had felt any bitterness towards a particular body and it confirmed my view that a prison record follows you everywhere.

In prison I had learned to love God in the silence

of my heart, for I had not been able to explore what I had felt with others. God alone had been my guide, for habits, tradition and protocol in these matters had not yet come my way. No one denomination had taken precedence over another, as the chapel had been used for every denomination. As far as I was concerned, God alone mattered; it was he whom all Christian people worshipped, and I was equally moved by worshipping him in Roman Catholic, Methodist, Quaker or Salvation Army services. As a result, I had come out of prison with no preconceived ideas on worship. Ecumenism, though virtually imposed by circumstances, really did work in prison, I felt.

Soon after my release I met one or two people with whom I could discuss fully my feelings on religion and God. During our discussions, I discovered divisions within the Christian family which saddened me, but it was also very exciting to discover others who had experienced a renewal of their own faith. We went for long, enjoyable walks debating theology, philosophy and life in general. Leaning against a gate or wall on summer evenings, watching the red glow of the sinking sun, and the changing light over a herd of cows, we contemplated God; in winter walking through the snow-filled lanes, we saw again the great beauty of his creation. Whatever the weather or the time of year, our thoughts turned often towards God, and I was aware of a heightened sense of spiritual freedom. Photography being something I love and missed in prison, I often took my camera along to try and capture those special moments.

When I had recovered from the shock of my parents' death, I returned to secretarial work, being careful not to mention that I had been in prison. At last I was earning a salary, and could begin to be self-sufficient.

Two years ago, at the time of writing, I was invited by a friend to join their party on a Greek island for a holiday. Because of my financial situation, I had not been able to have a holiday since leaving prison, but now the budget was just able to cope. I spent a blissful week living as part of the Greek Orthodox community. The days started with early morning prayer in the little cloistered, whitewashed monastery, five miles up the hill. We were greeted by a blaze of colour as we entered the gates. Blossom spilled over every wall and flowers grew in abundance from urns of all shapes and sizes. A small serene chapel stood in the middle of all this, and the sense of peace and God's presence was very powerful.

After the service, we were taken up to the refectory a couple of times to share some light refreshments. The only language spoken was Greek, but there was much happy laughter as cakes were generously handed round by the nuns. Our hosts picked and offered us small sprigs of scented jasmine blossom and Greek sweets to take away.

I was given permission to stay behind on one morning and, while the others returned to the villa, I went back into the little chapel and sat down in front of an icon of the Mother and Child, which was just inside the doorway. I became lost in stillness, awed by the mystery of God.

As I sat there, a Greek peasant woman came and stood beside me in front of the icon. She started praying and crying, then turned to me and began to tell me that she had lost her baby. She said that it had been her fault, and that she was unable to forgive herself. I could see why she had come to pray in front of this particular icon, for it had held me, too. I took her in my arms and spoke to her gently, trying to comfort her. She stayed with me for a while, then quietly left, while I continued to meditate, holding her in my prayers.

I shall never forget that day. I listened to the happy chatter of the nuns as they went about their daily routine – sweeping the courtyard, watering the flowers and quietly attending to the chapel – and found myself caught up in the peace and happiness.

Afterwards, I walked down the unmade track which had been carved into the hillside. Every now and then, I glimpsed a breathtaking view of the sea between the pines and the scrub. The colours all around me seemed to have intensified; they were brilliant and vivid. The heat seemed to magnify the sounds of the insects. The scent of pines, wild herbs, rocks, caked earth and sea mingled and filled the air.

On my return I told one of the others what had happened in the chapel. 'That's impossible,' she said, 'for you don't speak Greek, and she doesn't speak a word of English, so how did you understand?' This had not occurred to me until that moment. The only explanation I can give is that in worshipping God together in our hearts, language had ceased to be a barrier. In prayer we had become one, with a common language through the powerful presence of Christ. I later checked and verified the details of the story with a local family.

The next day we attended a celebration of the Eucharist in the chapel. I was very sad not to be able to take communion, particularly after what had just happened, but I respected their tradition which only allowed those within the denomination to participate. The woman whom I had met the day before was there. Our eyes met and, as she passed me on her way back from receiving communion, we gently hugged each other again, and I knew that something very special had taken place.

I came away from that holiday having experienced something of a deep spirituality within the Greek Orthodox Church. Grounded in tradition since the beginning of Christianity, their worship, I felt, was truly alive to the mysterious presence of God. I came away humbled that I had been given the privilege of worshipping with them and enriched beyond measure.

It was soon after this that it was suggested that I should share my story with others, so that they, too, might discover the joy and strength of God's love, even when life looks bleak. For a while I did not take up the suggestion, but I was given so much encouragement, that eventually I agreed to try and write a book. It seemed as though it was meant to be, for two things happened. I was beginning to suffer from high blood pressure, and needed a break from work; also, due to the money left to me on my parents' death, such a break was now financially possible.

Having the time to write gave me also the space to think, and be grateful for all that I have been given. I belong to a very loving church community, where I am able to be really involved. Gradually with their help, I have rediscovered the gift of laughter, for which I thank God – convinced that he has a sense of humour. Here I am accepted as 'Jenny', a person in my own right, and don't think of myself as an ex-offender but as just another member of the congregation. If some find it difficult to relate to what I have done, they have not made me aware of this. Their acceptance of me is something I treasure; it supports my belief in Jesus' teaching about love and forgiveness.

But the greatest treasure, God's forgiveness, drew me into a relationship with him that released guilt and brought about inner healing. The sense of wholeness and well-being which results is quite remarkable – something I would never have believed possible, if I had not experienced it for myself. This relationship with God has become the most exciting one that I have ever had.

In *Transformed By Love*, Sister Margaret Magdalen writes: 'Confession and healing are the only answer for painful memories.' She goes on to say, 'If through that healing there is also conversion, the memory is transfigured into a positive good. It becomes a tool which we can use in the service of others in their growth towards healing and wholeness.'

Our usefulness to others depends on and flows out of our relationship with God. Prayer is an important way of deepening that relationship into an intimate, personal friendship.

To try to return his love with mine, however feeble, gives me the courage to go on asking for his help and strength when I need it and praying that whatever the circumstances, it may be his

will, not mine, that prevails. In all this, I have a
spiritual friend who encourages and guides me along
the way, whose advice I value, especially perhaps
when things go wrong.

Sometimes I get a splinter embedded in my hand
when working in the garden. If I am to avoid having a
septic hand, I am likely to need someone else's help
in removing it and I will certainly need support if any
discomfort is involved. Similarly, I know my need of
the help, compassion and encouragement which God
gives, sometimes through others, in the removal of
life's splinters.

It is in our local church that the children and I have
made and dedicated a tapestry kneeler in memory
of Christopher. All of us have put in a stitch or two.
On Victoria's confirmation day she found herself
kneeling on that very same hassock. To know that
something we have made in his memory is used in
prayer week after week gives me a great sense of
peace. The simple picture on the hassock is of a
dove flying free from a cross. And that, it seems to
me, has been the movement of my life through pain
and suffering to joy and love; up from the depths
and into new life.

# POSTSCRIPT

For we know that in all things God works for the good of those who love him, who have been called according to his purpose.

*Romans 8: 28*

The tragic events that led to my being imprisoned were of my own doing and this often gives me a sense of embarrassment in the face of all the undeserved suffering around me in this world. But regardless of the circumstances which culminated in my being in prison, the pain, suffering and misery were real enough.

However, my experiences in prison and on my return home have left me utterly convinced of God's saving grace and his forgiving love. I may not always know what the future holds, but I am sure that it is in God's hands.

Having lived behind locked doors in a state of powerlessness, I value most the sense and tangible experience of freedom. Freedom to walk through the fields and woods once more. Freedom to make my own choices. Freedom to be open with my family and friends. Above all, the interior freedom which Christ gives me, for this does not rely on any material circumstances.

In order to cherish these freedoms and grow, I need times of solitude for prayer and, equally important, times of being with my family and friends. This is an essential balance to maintain, as it gives us all space to be ourselves, and to share our lives together happily. The children appreciate and value this freedom.

What I have in these two dimensions is beyond price, and my period of enforced deprivation, minimal comfort and personal possessions has enabled me to realise this. For I learned through prison life to live simply and to let life itself become my riches.

However, there were areas that I found quite devastating. One of these was the combination of loneliness and lack of privacy. The other was the sheer helplessness I felt at not being able to support and comfort the children. My imprisonment punished not just me, but all of us; and it was in this area that I felt guilt most keenly.

Despite all this, we have come through as a family. We can talk openly and freely. We speak of Christopher naturally, remembering the happy times we had together. Our house is often filled with laughter.

We are all aware that our lifestyle has changed dramatically, but compared to those who are homeless, hungry, lonely and depressed, we have riches that cannot be bought.

We have learned to appreciate the roof over our heads, the food we eat, the clothes we wear. More important than these things is the love we have for each other.

Since leaving prison, I have experienced a Christian fellowship which has given me the greatest joy. I have known rejection but can only look on this in a positive light for it has allowed me to relate more

fully to the many others who have, for whatever
reason, suffered the same fate.

As a child of ten or eleven, I took great pleasure in
writing stories. One was called 'The Blue Mountain',
and told of a knight in shining armour who had to get
to the top of the mountain to rescue a maiden.

Each side of the mountain was different. Danger-
ously rocky on one side, densely forested on another, sheer glass on a third, and a gentle grassy
slope on the fourth, it was also plagued with mon-
sters! There was only one way up. However feeble,
weak or strong you were, what got you to the top
was not intellect or physical prowess but 'love'.

I got my ideas from the endless fairy tales I
devoured at that time but, in a childlike, naïve way,
I had stumbled upon a truth in life, an attitude of
mind. For love can open our eyes to avenues which
under ordinary circumstances we cannot see.

I now find that fear is driven out by love; that
seemingly insurmountable problems become less
daunting when looked at gently in the light of love.

In a sense my spiritual journey began long before my conscious mind was aware of God. It
went on through the time when I knew about
him but couldn't be bothered with 'all that religious stuff'; it even continued while I was turning
my back on him until finally, from the bottom of
the heap, he picked me up and made me face
him.

Since then, it has not been a straightforward
or easy journey: sometimes I travel sideways or
even backwards; sometimes I need to pause, rest
or meditate before going on. But from wherever I
happen to be, the journey continues.

Now the more I see and think I understand, the more I realise how little I really know, and the more I try to comprehend God's mercy and love, the more I realise it is beyond me. I often think that if God can pick up a person such as myself, and give me the undeserved love that I have received, then no human being can be without hope.

In 1989 I was invited by the Board of Social Responsibility in the Salisbury diocese to attend a three-day conference in Lincoln on 'Human Values in Prisons'. It was heart-warming to see the concern for prisoners and to become aware of the efforts to rehabilitate and integrate them back into society and to explore alternatives to prisons as more constructive ways of dealing with particular crimes. However, I feel that initially we need to educate society to accept people from prison more readily!

That conference led to many doors being opened, and I have been invited back into several prisons. Without exception I have been humbled to see how God's Holy Spirit is moving in such unlikely environments. This should not be surprising for Jesus mixed with those whom society considered to be outcasts and he is still present in the midst of deprivation, suffering and loneliness.

After visiting one prison for a confirmation service, I was so elated that during the two-hour drive home I found myself spontaneously singing hymns of praise at the top of my voice.

Part of the journey was along the road from Bicester to Oxford where there is a vast programme of improvement works in operation causing long delays. I couldn't help laughing at the reactions of passing motorists who caught sight of me singing. The inner glow of joy remained long after my return home.

I am now involved with people in prison and their families. This wouldn't have been possible if I had not experienced prison life myself. I have become a member of the Prison Fellowship which, along with my own church community, supports me in what I do. This support is vital: to be of use to anyone, we need to recognise that we are part of the body of Christ and must never attempt to go it alone.

All this doesn't mean I am perfect or will not fail again and again. What I did seven years ago was very wrong, but I am convinced of salvation not through any merit from anything I might have done to try and put things right, but by God's free gift of grace, and I hope I am able to share this with others who find themselves in similar situations.

On Monday of Holy Week 1990 I took a tumble down the stairs and was in terrible pain for nearly a fortnight. The only place where I could rest with a certain degree of comfort was on my prayer stool. In that position, I was mercilessly ragged!

However, sitting there, I was able to contemplate the passion of our Lord. I thought of the pain that the two thieves were also experiencing as they hung on either side of Jesus. While one hurled insults, the other recognised Jesus for who he was and even in his agony, turned to him for forgiveness.

'Today,' Jesus replied, 'you will be with me in paradise' (Luke 23).

I can identify with that thief. I, too, have been forgiven. On the basis of that forgiveness, God has transformed my life and given me inner peace and quiet happiness. I can therefore echo William Temple's words:

> The fully forgiven man does not rejoice in his own forgiveness, but in the divine love to which he owes it; and his past sin persists in his experience no longer as a source of shame, but as the occasion of a new wonder in his adoration of the love divine.

Hodder Christian Paperbacks: a tradition of excellence.

Great names and great books to enrich your life and meet your needs. Choose from such authors as:

| | |
|---|---|
| **Corrie ten Boom** | **Jackie Pullinger** |
| **Charles Colson** | **David Pytches** |
| **Richard Foster** | **Mary Pytches** |
| **Billy Graham** | **Jennifer Rees Larcombe** |
| **Michael Green** | **Cliff Richard** |
| **Michele Guinness** | **John Stott** |
| **Joyce Huggett** | **Joni Eareckson Tada** |
| **Francis MacNutt** | **Colin Urquhart** |
| **Catherine Marshall** | **David Watson** |
| **Jim Packer** | **David Wilkerson** |
| **Adrian Plass** | **John Wimber** |

The wide range of books on the Hodder Christian Paperback list include biography, personal testimony, devotional books, evangelistic books, Christian teaching, fiction, drama, poetry, books that give help for times of need – and many others.

Ask at your nearest Christian bookshop or at your church bookstall for the latest titles.

# SOME BESTSELLERS IN HODDER CHRISTIAN PAPERBACK

### THE HIDING PLACE by Corrie ten Boom

The triumphant story of Corrie ten Boom, heroine of the anti-Nazi underground.

"A brave and heartening story."

*Baptist Times*

### GOD'S SMUGGLER by Brother Andrew

An international besteller. God's Smuggler carries contraband Bibles past armed border guards to bring the love of Christ to the people behind the Iron Curtain.

"A book you will not want to miss."

*Catherine Marshall*

### DISCIPLESHIP by David Watson

" . . . breath-taking, block-busting, Bible-based simplicity on every page."

*Jim Packer*

### LISTENING TO GOD by Joyce Huggett

A profound spiritual testimony, and practical help for discovering a new dimension of prayer.

"This is counselling at its best."

*Leadership Today*

### CELEBRATION OF DISCIPLINE by Richard Foster

A classic on the Spiritual Disciplines.

"For any Christian hungry for teaching, I would recommend this as being one of the most challenging books to have been published."

*Delia Smith*

### RUN BABY RUN by Nicky Cruz with Jamie Buckingham

A tough New York gang leader discovers Christ.

"It is a thrilling story. My hope is that it shall have a wide reading."

*Billy Graham*

### CHASING THE DRAGON by Jackie Pullinger with Andrew Quicke

Life-changing miracles in Hong Kong's Walled City.

"A book to stop you in your tracks.'

*Liverpool Daily Post*

### BORN AGAIN by Charles Colson

Disgraced by Watergate, Charles Colson finds a new life.

"An action packed story of real life drama and a revelation of modern history as well as a moving personal account."

*Elim Evangel*

**KNOWING GOD by J I Packer**

The biblical portrait that has become a classic.

"(The author) illumines every doctrine he touches and commends it with courage, logic, lucidity and warmth ... the truth he handles fires the heart. At least it fired mine, and compelled me to turn aside to worship and pray."

*John Stott*

**THE HAPPIEST PEOPLE ON EARTH by Demos Shakarian with John and Elizabeth Sherrill**

The extraordinary beginnings of the Full Gospel Business Men's Fellowship.